A Wake-up Call

Sandra Colin

© 2024 by Sandra Colin

Scriptures marked KJV are taken from the KING JAMES VERSION (KJV): KING JAMES VERSION, public domain.

All rights reserved. This book or any portion thereof may not be reproduced or used in any manner whatsoever without the express written permission of the publisher except for the use of brief quotations in a book review.

Cover design by Hanah

Interior design by Amina N. (To contact: aminanaveed794@gmail.com)

First Printing, 2024

ISBN 978-1-7382414-3-9

Printed in Canada.

Table Of Contents

Acknowledgements 5

Chapter 1… Childhood 8

Chapter 2… A Home Away From Home 17

Chapter 3… Back To My Roots 26

Chapter 4… Naïveté 50

Chapter 5… Marriage 62

Chapter 6… Divorce 87

Lessons Of Mine 115

Epilogue 120

Works Cited 122

Acknowledgements

I sincerely would like to thank Jesus first for motivating me to write this story. He inspired me to write it in the first place. Moreover, He was the One who saved me in the first place. He used people to inform me that this book was my calling. I would like to name one of them, because I know her name. She was my mentor. God used her to lift me up, when I was going through hard trials. Her name is Anne Latour. I love her.

I would like to thank the individuals who God used to push me towards the completion of this book. I love every one of these individuals. During the writing process of this book, there were a lot of phone calls even in the night when I was lying down in bed. I did not recognize a single phone number of theirs. They did not transpire until I notified a certain community that I would be releasing a book. The enemy was attacking me through repetitive phone calls from a certain stranger. Nevertheless, I knew that it was a distraction from writing this book because of the frequency and timing of the phone calls and from whom they came. Before then, I did not know that this book would be such a threat to the kingdom of darkness.

I would like to thank my dad for taking care of my children and I. I am so grateful for the food that he gave us and other items. He provided things for me during my time of healing. Thank

You, God, for using my father to help me accomplish what I needed to do!

I would like to thank my mother for buying things like clothing and other items for the children and I throughout our lives. They are much appreciated. I am grateful for the times in which my mother joked around. She made me laugh a lot. Thank You, God, for giving me a mother that gave me the gift of life.

CHAPTER 1

CHILDHOOD

The only four memories of mine that remain of my parents, when they shared a romantic relationship with each other, are the following.

The First Memory

My dad, my mom, and I were sitting at a table in the dining room. My mom had dirty blond hair. My dad naturally possessed red hair. He was very handsome. My dad swiftly lifted a big, plastic, white bowl, as he rose from his chair. So, popcorn went flying out of it.

The Second Memory

This was a bunch of memories that are a blur of repetition. My parents would argue with each other. As I would cry, I would slide down the wall with my back against the wall from a standing position down to a squatting position and, then, down onto my ankles.

The Third Memory

My dad and my mom were approaching each other from opposite ends of a room and I walked to a spot in between them. Then, I stood there and blocked them from each other with outstretched arms, as if I was pushing them away from each other. Nevertheless, my hands were not touching them.

"No," I said.

The Fourth Memory

My mother, my dad and I were at home.

"Let's go," my mom said, near the front door. My dad was sitting nowhere near the front door. I froze in a standing position. Eventually, I followed her through the doorway and we left our home. This event's trauma led me to believe that I was the one who occasioned my parents to separate. I believed that I should not have spoken up. I had done so, when they were approaching each other from different directions. Though they had not argued once more in my presence since then, they did separate from each other shortly thereafter. Therefore, I did not want to speak anymore. This occurred when I was nearing five years young. We did not dwell in that apartment again. My mom remained separated from him until she was legally divorced from him. Nevertheless, I spent time with my dad on every second weekend and on Wednesdays.

While I spent time with my mom, I missed my dad. While I was in the presence of my dad, I missed my mom's presence. I shed a great deal of tears over their separation. *Life is no longer the same*, I thought.

Playground

When I was five years of age, my mom and I strolled to a playground. I possessed short, reddish brown hair. It looked like a bowl haircut. I jumped on the swing and I sat on it. No sand existed under the swing, but, instead, there was dry, hard cement. I fell on the cement.

On another day, we strolled by the same playground. My mom was heading in the direction of the houses nearby, which would lead us away from the playground. Nevertheless, I mounted the swing. Then, I fell onto the cement ground, hitting my head. So, I ended up in the hospital. (What happened to my head, God discerns. My mom and my dad related conflicting stories to me. My dad said that my head had cracked open. My mom denied this.)

Home Life

Throughout my life, in general, when I liked or loved something or someone (and when I told my stepdad so), he either would touch on it (as if it was evil), or he would say that he despised it. So, I feared being myself. I would pretend to not like what I liked. I would pretend to hate what I liked. I would seek to conceal my likes and dislikes from Luc, my stepdad. Moreover, my stepdad hated children.

My stepdad had black, wavy hair. It was somewhat short. Oftentimes, he grew it out a little or so at the nape of the neck.

Luc handed me gifts on my birthday while I lived with him. They oftentimes were VHS tapes of movies because I was a movie junkie.

Oftentimes, my mom looked at me with a suspicious look on her face, when I spoke my mind on things. She would speak, as if she considered the opinion or I evil. Nevertheless, sometimes, she spoke to me in a polite manner. Throughout most of my life, I was inseparable from my mother.

My mom and Luc spoke in French to each other at home because French was their maternal tongue. When I spoke in French to them, they replied in English. English was my first language, but French was a close second language of mine.

My mom, Luc, and even sometimes my father would kill my joy whenever I would express excitement and/or joy in their presence. My mother would look at me suspiciously if I did so.

My father, my mother and Luc would continually contradict me. The gaslighting did negatively affect me over time. As an adult, I doubted my memories, my judgment, etc. I lived my life asking my dad and my mom or others what I should execute. Moreover, I suffered from self-doubt.

My dad suffered from alcoholism. So, he did not give me much time to utter words before cutting me off. That happened oftentimes before I finished my first sentence. Then, he would ask me a query. He treated me as if he considered me dumb. Moreover, he behaved in angry outbursts at times. At other times, he treated me politely. He generously provided money and other objects to me. He commanded me to not smoke and paid me for abstaining from smoking. Nevertheless, he puffed on cigarettes.

He oftentimes had hostility in his eyes, when I fixed my eyes on his eyes. Moreover, he falsely accused me of executing misdeeds throughout my life.

Nevertheless, throughout most of my life, I was chummy with my dad. My father had compassion on me at times and accommodated me. For example, if I felt cold, he would turn off a fan. He also stood up for me from time to time when it was needed.

On one evening, I was staying at my babysitter's place. She was playing the film, *Chucky*, on TV. A scene with Chucky freaked me out. So, I strode away from the TV screen. Following the completion of the babysitting period, I reported this event to my mom. I informed her that I had experienced fear from that film. Therefore, the babysitter never babysat me anew.

When I was five years old, I began to masturbate. This may have occurred after I had viewed the movie, Pumping Iron.

"Don't talk to strangers," my mother said to me, while we were outdoors.

"Okay," I said. I was five years young. In a little while, I stepped up the black steps of a yellow school bus. It was my first time, heading off to school.

Each morning, when I would arrive at Pleasant Park Public school, there was hot chocolate in the cafeteria. Therefore, I sat at a table. I gradually drank a cup of it with marshmallows, as it warmed me up. It tasted so delectable.

On Fridays, students had access to pizza at the cafeteria. So, I gave a toonie for it well ahead of time and, then, my cheese pizza arrived on Fridays.

When I turned seven years of age, I was with a babysitter of mine and another girl. The other girl was younger than I and small. I said something inappropriate. I do not know recall what it was.

Then, on another day, the mother came by and had a present in her lap. She held it like she wanted to give me the present.

"Did you say –"? she said. I do not recall the rest of what she expressed.

"No," I lied. Then, she handed me the gift. I took it. Nevertheless, I felt that I did not deserve the gift. She appeared to believe me instead of her own child. I felt guilty about lying and having said what I had said to the girl. From that moment onward, I believed that I would not be a good mom. Therefore, I feared that I would become a mom. Nevertheless, at times, I still desired to have my own children.

Gaping Slash

When I was 7 or 8 years old, I developed appendicitis. It manifested as noticeable pain in my abdomen. I was eating a tiny amount of nourishment day after day, because I did not possess an appetite. Then, I was transported by car to a hospital. My dad and my mom accompanied me to the emergency section of the hospital. I waited there all night as the pain worsened. It was so intense that I started to moan. My dad felt helpless. He was clueless as to how to aid me. At about 6 a.m., the doctor arrived.

Then, after a little bit, I went into a secluded room. I was put to sleep by sleeping gas. Then, the surgery took place. When I awoke, my abdomen had a gaping slash on the right side. I peered to the right through a window and spotted a black sky. All that I saw was blackness outside of the window. It was midnight. Neither a band-aid nor a single other thing was on the wound. At one point, someone told me that my appendix had burst, and, then, it had been removed by this surgery. During my days in the hospital, my dad coaxed me to walk in the hallway. Walking was tender, but the exercise of my limbs strengthened me. In a public space, I spent time, discovering how to sew during my two-week stay. I had never sewn a thing before then. I sewed two brown felt sheets together and they were cut in the outline of a rabbit.

I returned to school, and on the first day in a certain classroom, many students formed a circle around me and simultaneously gave me a hug. I felt so treasured.

During my time living on Sandalwood Drive, my mother and I would bike together to a certain mall. We would bike on some grassy fields and, then, up a grassy, small incline. We did not own a car. So, we travelled by car, or by bus, or by foot during most of my childhood. I enjoyed travelling on my pink bike and my mother enjoyed cycling, too.

While I was in the fifth grade, Leah asked me if she could sleep over at my place. She had been my close friend since I was five years young. She had short, brown hair and pale skin.

A curse word escaped my mom's boyfriend's lips. He called me a profane name. His name was Luc. He had formed a plan involving my mom.

He had been dwelling with us since I was five years young.

Goodbye

My mom talked about her desire to move to Québec. That is where her friend, Linda, relocated to. "You're going to regret moving to Québec," Luc said. "Just wait and see."

It was the last day of school for that cyclical school year of mine in the fifth grade at Pleasant Park Public School. After our classes were over, people were running a race on a track. So, I joined in for the next one. There were some fun activities that many students and I participated in.

On the day when Luc, my mom, and I took off from Ottawa, Ontario by car, we started to cross a bridge. Luc excitedly yelled something, driving the car. I did not feel excitement, because I was leaving my close friend and other friends behind. My soul fragmented. Nevertheless, I pretended to feel excitement, and I tried to feel it.

This was the first time in my life since my mother moved out of my father's place in which one of our household members owned a car.

CHAPTER 2

A HOME AWAY FROM HOME

We relocated to a short apartment building in Aylmer, Québec.

In the summertime, I stayed and slept in a bunk bed at Camp Davern. My bedroom was in a cabin. There were affable people and amusing activities for children at this camp. Some activities were facultative, but others were mandatory. During a hike with fellow campers and our guides, I detected minuscule frogs at the side of the footpath in the forest. They were the smallest frogs that I had ever seen. They were a third of the size of my little finger. I held different ones one at a time in my hand. Then, they leaped off of my hand.

Once while traversing a road, I spotted a crushed snake. After crossing the road, I approached it and squatted. Part of its pink guts were hanging out of the snake in the areas, where it had been crushed. I desired to aid it, but I felt helpless. Then, a car came by and ran over it. "No!" I said.

St. Mark's

I commenced the sixth grade at St. Mark's Public School in Québec. I did not recognize anyone there. Nevertheless, I regularly frequented the company of a group of three girls for weeks. Each of them usually wore an 8-inch high backpack on her back. It was the 90s. So, they were on trend. I did not own this type of backpack. So, I was not wearing one. One of the girls was named Roxanne. She had medium-length, red hair. Becky was towering for her age. She was taller than I even though I was tall for my age. Chantal was not as tall as Roxanne, who was not as tall as I. Chantal had dark brown hair and Becky had short, red hair. Our teacher gave our class an assignment. So, the four of us discussed the presentation and concurred on presenting a certain Spice Girls' song in our classroom.

"When will we practice together?" I asked Roxanne. She said that she would inform me of the date. The appointed time came for us to do the class presentation of a Spice Girls' song. The music played, then, they began to dance to it in synchronicity. Their dancing astonished me because they had not practiced these moves with me beforehand. Moreover, I had not been notified by a single one of them that they were intending to dance during this presentation. Nevertheless, I swiftly matched their moves while watching them.

Embarrassment

On one day, I was sitting at a desk with a vertical partition, blocking part of Roxanne from view. I wrote a note on a tiny piece of lined paper and slid it on the desk to Roxanne. It said,

"Gata is very attractive." Gata was a tall boy in our class, who possessed light-brown skin. She read the note.

"Come, see," Roxanne said, motioning. The whole remainder of the class came over and viewed the note, including Gata. I felt abashed.

On a school day, Roxanne, the two other girls in our group, and I were outside at recess. Roxanne approached me.

"You can't continue hanging out with us because Becky doesn't want you to," Roxanne said. "I'm sorry."

Afterwards, I sought to hang out with different people at recess. At one point, I wept. Nevertheless, one group of two girls was approachable.

"Are you okay?" a boy said. His name was Jesse. He had, short dark brown hair and pale skin.

"Yeah," I said. "I'm okay." Then, he left my presence. A little bit afterwards, I ferreted for him in order to inform him of why I had been crying. Nevertheless, I did not find him in the recess area, which mostly was a courtyard. I hung out with a group of people, who were younger than I. Nevertheless, they treated me courteously.

One group of two girls were affable and they were the same age as I. Nevertheless, I felt like I had nothing to affix to their conversations. Therefore, I felt uninterested while we were in a circle, as they conversed with each other.

I spoke to Leah, my close friend, over the phone. I told her how I longed to see her and I did not have close friends in Aylmer, Québec.

In the hallway of our school, I was interacting with a brunette. She was a classmate of mine.

"If you want to make friends, you're going to have to start talking," she said. I had often behaved in a mute manner in social situations and in general. I held that I had nothing engaging to converse about. I oftentimes expressed more through my eyes and through my body language than through my speech.

On one day, Jesse came over to the table, that I had seated myself at. Then, he started to stare at me. I felt ill at ease with the ogle. When Jesse turned his face away from me, I printed on our table, "Jesse is queer." Jesse reported the incident to the English teacher. She had short, light-brown hair, and her name was Mrs. Patrick. I thought, *Some people recognize the writing and think that it is my handwriting because I correct things with a blue pen. They recognize the letter, "I" and the writing is facing me. Everyone knows it was me, except for Stefan and Ricky.* Mrs. Patrick instructed me that I had to reveal to certain people that I had written the message. The teacher also indicated, I had to apologize to Jesse so that I would not incur more trouble. So, I told Sophia, Kristine, and Emilia that I had written the message. Then, while Jesse was sitting on a bench in a gym, I approached him. Then, I confessed my sin against him, and I apologized for it. Nevertheless, he responded with a heated look.

Now, all I had to do was notify my mom about it so that she would not be taken aback by a phone call. When I went to my gym class, I thought, *At least, Mr. Ben does not know about it for now anyways and he is still nice to me.* He was my teacher. I wrote in my diary, "Today, November 2, 1997 has been the worst day of my life and I mean the worst."

In December, I won a prize for enunciating words in French.

"She doesn't even speak," Lisa said. Then, I harboured unforgiveness towards her for that comment. She wore a silver cuff earring on the outside curve of cartilage in the outer ear. She had wavy, dark brown hair and Lisa tended to wear a white sweatband on each of her wrists.

Once the sixth grade ended, I attended Grande Rivière. It was a high school that was composed of the seventh grade all the way up to the eleventh grade. This system was reserved for Québec. It differed from the other provinces in Canada. On my first day at Grande Rivière, a girl came up to me and started conversing with me. Nevertheless, the conversation was short. Then she raced away to another person. Other girls approached me one-by-one and chatted with me. Then, they raced away from me and communicated to another person.

I made a bunch of friends in the beginning, but the friendships did not turn into company at lunch time on a daily basis. I sought someone to hang out with at lunch time. Nevertheless, I did not find one that lasted. One person hung out with me at lunch time on some days, but she smoked. She smoked a cigarette, as we walked side-by-side, or as we stood near one another at lunchtime. I started to feel the temptation to smoke. So, I decided to discontinue hanging out with her.

On one day, after I had eaten my lunch, I strolled into a hallway at the school.

"You can make friends with them," a lady said, pointing at a group of girls nearby. "They speak English." I felt that I should not need aid with getting acquainted with new friends. Pride prevented me from approaching those girls.

Three days in a row, I consumed my lunch in a bathroom stall. I did so to avoid the ingestion of it solo at a table in the cafeteria. On the third day in which I executed this act, I came out of the washroom. Then, I dropped the garbage into the garbage receptacle. A guy angrily yelled at me, but I did not catch what he was uttering. I was in shock that he was angrily hollering at me in French. I tended to not catch what people said when they yelled things. Trauma brought that about. I felt fear, when I heard shouting. Moreover, people in Québec tended to eat their words, when they spoke in French.

He was a stranger and he looked like he was a student there. I simply walked away.

During the months in which I attended Grande Rivière, my mother rarely conversed with me. Instead, she spent time lying in her bed. Once I begged her to talk to me. Then, she sat and

talked to me. We communicated with each other in English. Luc did not communicate with me in an affable manner. So, I felt quite dejected from the lack of escort. Once when I stood in the hallway of the school, I unclosed my mouth to utter something, but no sound was emitted from it. I had aimed to speak, but my throat had felt dry.

On one day, students and I were seated in a classroom while a teacher was present. Our teacher instructed a boy to execute a certain task.

I had spotted this boy at St. Mark's Public School. He had been physically assaulted by two boys at the school, as they had pushed him up against a fence.

At this moment, he walked up to the front of the classroom and spoke in French in front of the green chalkboard. He had blond, slightly long, and wavy hair. When he enunciated French words, I perceived a Canadian English accent. Some other boys jeered at him and laughed at him. I watched, horrified by their treatment of this boy. This event fragmented my soul.

On one day in the seventh grade, our class was seated and the teacher put on a movie. The opening scene showed people at someone's front door. One man spoke at the door, holding a plate of food. Another man was watching for him at the front door. They were trying to coax the person to open the door, but that did not transpire. Then, one of these men opened the door and saw evidence on the grey-haired man's wrist that he was in the act of suicide. This scene fragmented my soul and made me experience fear. This scene was part of the film, Amadeus.

When the February school break was approaching, I thought, *This is my chance to leave this school for good*. I went over to my dad's apartment and tried to remain in Ottawa, Ontario past the completion of the break. That did not last. Somehow, I ended up back at my mom's apartment in Aylmer, Québec. On another occasion, when I was at my home in Québec, I grasped a knife out of a drawer. It was a serrated paring knife. Then, I put it back in the drawer, and I called my dad on the phone.

"Hey, Dad," I said. "Look. I don't want to live here anymore. I took a knife out of the drawer to kill myself. But I did not do that, because I fear seeing myself bleed." My dad came over the next day to pick me up. At some point, my dad worked something out with Leah's parents. My dad pretended that he lived in the catchment area of Vincent Massey Public School. So, I returned to his apartment and attended a new school. This apartment building was dark brown on the exterior, and it was composed of many floors. It was in Ottawa, Ontario. I dwelt there for a week and a half. Then, my mom turned up at our door. I am not cognizant of all the details. Nevertheless, I know that the following occurred. The police arrived at our front door.

"You got to come now," the police said. I was lying down on my stomach on the carpet. "You got to get up and go." I rose from the carpet and exited my dad's apartment. Luc was watching for our arrival outside in the car. Then, I entered his car and put on a seat belt. Then, Luc steered the car, as I was seated in it. So, we retroceded to our dwelling in Aylmer.

CHAPTER 3

BACK TO MY ROOTS

Soon thereafter, my mom, Luc, and I moved to a high-rise in Ottawa, Ontario. Then, I continued to attend Vincent Massey Public School, which Leah attended. I desired to be in the same class as her. By then, Leah's hair had grown into long, wavy hair. She was in the Core French program. So, instead of going into the Gifted French program (which I was eligible for), I entered the Core French program. Nevertheless, I found it so boring because it was too easy. It touched on information that I was well acquainted with. I was moving from an all-French program at Grande Rivière to a Core French program.

My mom said that she had been experiencing chronic fatigue, while we had been living in Aylmer. She had spent time at her mother's place resting and recuperating. She said that all the traveling from her home in Aylmer, Québec to her workplace in Ottawa, Ontario had exhausted her. She had been working as a home care worker.

When I started to interact with other students at lunchtime at Vincent Massey Public School, they treated me warmly, incorporating Leah. Almost none of the students (that had attended Pleasant Park Public School) attended that school. The exceptions were Leah and Jonathan.

In August, I went out with my mom to a store. I was looking for hair spray, but I was not succeeding in finding some. Then, I chose some make-up. Whatever I chose my mom said, "You don't need make-up," or "It'll cause zits to break out and it doesn't let your skin breathe." My mom said that she did not possess sufficient money for make-up and hair spray. So, she purchased nothing but some hair spray in a can.

Then, we went home, although we had purposed to head to the YMCA-YWCA. The plan had been that we would go swimming. The other part of the arrangement had been that my mom would do a workout. Nevertheless, I had not felt like heading there afterwards. Moreover, my mom did not manage to find her bathing suit. I did not want to enter the YMCA-YWCA building and merely do a workout (or split up and I would go swimming solo while she did her workout). *It is out of the question*, I thought. My mom said that she was not intending to buy a bathing suit because she did not have sufficient money.

"Do you want to go see a movie?" my mom said.

"Sure," I said. "Why not?" So, we looked in the papers and decided to see *The Haunting*. It was a horror film that was rated PG. So, we headed off to the cinema. We entered our assigned room. It was dark. Nevertheless, we found seats and sat beside each other. Then, the ads for other films came. Lastly, our film came on. *The horror scenes in the film aren't so fake*, I thought. It turned out to be an excellent movie. When the movie ended, we foraged through the hallways of the cinema building, looking for Luc. I went outside to see if he was there. Nevertheless, I did not spot him nor his car anywhere. I went to both ends of the cinema, seeking him. Nevertheless, I did not spot him nor his car. We waited for one hour and 50 minutes, while we were standing. Then, we called my dad at around 11:30 p.m. (and we had been waiting since 10:10 p.m.).

"Oh, there he is – my saviour," I said, spotting my dad's car at the front of the cinema. He picked us up, and we arrived at home at 12:00 a.m. I got ready for bed and we listened to a few audio messages on our answering machine. The first one consisted of my mom, calling Luc. The second one consisted of Luc, phoning our apartment to see if we were at home. The third message consisted of my dad, phoning Luc to inform him that he was picking us up (in the event that he was sleeping).

Luc entered our home.

"Where were you guys?" Luc said. "I was waiting for you for three hours. I was there since 10:05 p.m." We had neither spotted him at the cinema building nor in the parking lot nor anywhere else.

"Where have you been?" I said.

"Right in front of the building," Luc said.

"Were you at the left or at the right of it?" I said.

"At the left side," he said. He still owned a car, but, soon afterwards, he no longer owned one.

Out Of The Blue

A bunch of girls rushed up to me outside and behind our school.

"Liban wants you to become his girlfriend," they said. Liban had dark brown skin. He was tall for his age. I thought, *This is not the appropriate time for him to court me. I am just a young child. Moreover, this guy is not acquainted with me.*

"Really?" I said, eyeing them.

"Yes, he does," they said.

"Okay," I said. "I'll be his girlfriend." I gave my approval out of the fear of rejection from them, if I would have said no. Then, they rushed away from me. On one day, Liban came up to me and gave me a peck on the cheek. I replicated the same gesture on his cheek. Then, he walked away. There was an occasion, in which I was conversing with him outside in the courtyard at the back of the school. I suggested that we head to a gathering of our friends at a certain person's residence. Then, his face changed to a heated facial expression and he did not utter a word.

We almost never interacted with one another. Then, some weeks subsequently, some girls approached me.

"Liban is breaking up with you," they said. They said that he did not like me any longer. *He never liked me,* I thought. *He only liked my beauty.* I started to tear up a bit after I spotted him looking at me. I never looked at him for long again except in hatred. I walked away and held my tears back. I thought, *I have done something wrong, but I had not done a thing that would have caused this to happen. I just had been thinking that he would never leave me. I had thought that he was planning to marry me.* I started walking towards the basketball nets that were near the parking lot. Everald and a tall guy were playing basketball. So, I sat down on the ground and observed them. I sought Leah because I needed her to comfort me. Emily and Leah were riding their bicycles nearby. I started to cry, but I hung my head down so that I could obscure the teary look of mine. But Emily returned and inquired what was wrong. I related the tale to her.

"I warned you that he would dump you," she said. "He broke my heart three times." *She's right,* I thought. *When she had warned me, I should have believed her. I should have taken her warning seriously and not continued the relationship. I should have never started the relationship in the first place. She is being nice for once. Nevertheless, she is still my enemy.* Then, Leah returned to the courtyard on her bicycle and she dismounted from her bicycle.

"I'm very sorry," Leah said. I cried a lot and loudly, as I was sitting on the ground.

"Everald, come over here and give Sandra a hug." I felt slightly ill at ease about her request. I thought, *The hug will be artificial*. Then, he gave me a hug.

A little afterwards, another dark-skinned guy said that he liked me. He was the one who I had been watching. He had been playing basketball. I smiled, eyeing him.

"Not another one," Leah said. She was reacting in jealousy towards me.

On another school day, my group of friends were outside of Vincent Massey Public School during recess, and I accompanied them.

"We don't want you hanging out with us," Pam said. She was an obese girl with long, blond hair. She kept her hair in a low, slicked-back ponytail.

"Is that true?" I said, looking at the group of girls. "Do you not want me to hang out with you"? I said.

"No," one of the girls said. "That's not true."

On some days, I heard name calling in the hallway by Melissa. Melissa had long, blond, and wavy hair. She was slender. The hallway was almost empty and she was meters away from me. She walked way behind me, and, in former days, we had conversed in an amicable manner. So, I was puzzled.

One day, Pam started to call me derogatory names and started to use swear words in a classroom within earshot of our teacher. The teacher was instructing a lesson, while Pam, and the other students were seated in chairs. The female teacher did not correct Pam's behaviour, while I was present. She acted as if it was not occurring. This railing went on each school day for a month. I walked home crying day after day. I informed my dad about it.

"Punch her in the nose," he said.

"No," I said. "I don't want to hit her." On another occasion, I narrated this account to my mom.

"Go to your principal," she said. "Tell her about it." So, on one day, I met up with the principal and informed her of the offensive, vulgar name calling by Pamela and Melissa. I do not want to incorporate the words that they uttered. Some of what was said were swear words. Then, on another day, the principal called all three of us to a convocation with her. She asked the two girls why they were treating me in such a way. After that meeting, Pam stopped swearing at me and calling me offensive names, and Melissa stopped calling me offensive names regarding one's sexual lifestyle.

By the way, I was a virgin.

On one occasion, some male friends and I formed a half-circle at school. The teenage boys were conversing with one another, and a male student pushed a ruler in between my buttocks' cheeks from behind me. His name was Brett. He was not taller than the average boy for his age to put it mildly. The stick did not penetrate a thing. Nevertheless, I immediately wept, with tears streaming down my cheeks. None of the guys emitted a word about it. No one queried me as to what I was bewailing.

After that event, I developed a fear of men and of boys.

An Application

I informed my dad that Canterbury High School was not in my catchment area.

"Do you really want to go there?" Dad asked.

"Yes," I said. I longed to go to this high school, as Jen intended to attend the high school. Jen had light-brown hair and she wore it in a shoulder-length bob. She was my intimate friend at Vincent Massey Public School.

The day came when I tarried in the hallway of Canterbury High School and an adolescent girl approached me. Then, she embraced me, though she was a stranger to me. Then, she strolled away from me without saying a word. Then, I was ushered into a secluded room. A man shut the door from which I entered. He instructed me to sing. So, I sang a song. After my audition, he notified me that I had not been accepted into the vocal arts program.

Nevertheless, I applied to the school, inserting my dad's home address as mine in the application form. Then, I received admittance into the non-specialized arts program at the high school. This school was within the walking distance of 20 minutes from my dwelling, where my mom resided. Nevertheless, I took an OC Transpo bus to wind up at school in the morning.

Dances frequently took place at the school. On some months, one could attend a dance weekend after weekend. My friends attended dances there. So, I participated in them. I relished the music and became more at ease with dancing there, as time progressed. I could dance there for hours. *The music is terrific*, I was thinking. It was blasting from a loudspeaker. It gave you the feel of being at a concert with your favourite artist.

Nevertheless, on one of those occasions, while my friends and I were in the hallway at the dancehall, I spotted two teenage girls French kissing each other. I pointed this act out to Jennifer.

"They're just friends," she said.

When I was attending Canterbury High School, I attended a class that included a module on women's self-defense.

Then, outside of the classroom, I informed a man that I had grasped how to defend myself in diverse situations. I showed the man what I had imbibed. Nevertheless, the man commenced to choke me. I used a certain approach (which I had learned in the class) to break a choke hold. Nevertheless, his grip did not break off of my neck and it did not lessen. What did lessen was my oxygen intake. Some seconds later, he stopped choking me. I remained conscious during the choking and in the aftermath.

"Why did you choke me?" I said. I do not remember his reply. He did not show repentance for what he had executed.

On one day, I was in a science classroom, the teacher taught us the Big Bang Theory. It was the first time that I had heard it. Then, a guy raised his hand.

"Yes?" the teacher said.

"Creation is a theory of how things came to be. Why don't you teach about creation as a source of life on Earth?" the adolescent boy said.

After the class ended, I asked this boy about this matter. His name was Greg. I asked him to explain the theory. He just said that he had wanted the teacher to teach on creation. I was displeased about his response. I was so curious about this theory that Greg touched on. I just wanted to know more about it.

I was on the sidewalk in front of our school, and a bus stop was nearby. There was a bus shelter near it, which included a brown bench. The bus shelter was made of glass. I stood there, and spotted a girl near me. She had short, light-brown hair that reached a little past her chin. She started to converse with me. She became my most intimate friend, and her name was Natasha.

She invited me to her residence. She lived in a rural area, but I lived in an urban setting. Nevertheless, I accepted the invitation. I arrived at her dwelling and she introduced me to a certain board game. She told me to place my fingers on the rectangular device and she used the same technique. We posed queries to whom I did not know. The rectangular, white device moved, though we were not pushing it. It moved to different characters on the board. Either, some entity dragged it to the words, "yes," "no," or to a letter.

"Who will be my husband"? I said. It gave an answer, starting with two consonants. *This is not accurate*, I thought. *Nevertheless, it's harmless like an 8-Ball.* It was a Ouija board. I do not remember the queries that Natasha put forward.

Natasha and I conversed on the phone per diem. We talked for an hour or more per conversation. We related to each other so well, and her words made me laugh oftentimes. She often named me "babe."

One day, she accompanied me to my maternal grandmother's place, which was in the countryside. It was not in the same rural town, where Natasha lived. My grandmother's house was in Alexandria. It possessed a yellow exterior. We played with the Ouija board right on the dining room table, and we possessed no remorse about it. This was my Ouija board, since my mom had bought me one.

In those days, I was practicing yoga and drinking one glass of Pepsi before my bedtime.

I read about yoga's spiritual nature in a Shape magazine. The concept of the improvement of one's spirituality (through yoga) intrigued me. So, I started complying with the instructions of a yoga instructor on a VHS tape, as I watched it on a TV screen in the living room. Then, I continued to pursue it daily, since it made the muscles in my body loosen. Therefore, I felt carefree. Nevertheless, I was having difficulty with reaching dormancy at night. I was getting a scanty amount of sleep in the hours of darkness. On one night, I only had slept for three hours, but I still attended school in the morning and in the afternoon.

Onset

One night, I went with my dad to a rock concert in Toronto on a Sunday night. *He is more interested in it than I am*, I thought. We watched diverse groups, and some soloists, perform onstage. I did not recognize one of the vocalists, because I did not recall seeing him somewhere before then. Nevertheless, my dad perceived who he was. He was Bruce Cockburn. We were sitting on chairs during the whole concert. One of the performers dishonored the musical group, The Backstreet Boys. Some people booed and my dad looked over at me with a look that showed pity in a scornful way. It was not compassionate. I was a Backstreet Boys fan then, and I had been one since I was 10 years young. A little while afterwards, an episode of heart arrhythmia started out of the blue. This was the first occasion in which I experienced heart arrhythmia. My heart was palpitating.

"My heart is racing so fast," I said. "I want it to stop." My dad and I rose from our chairs and exited the concert room. Then, my dad bought a black T-shirt in the corridor, and the T-shirt read, "Music Without Borders." That was the title of the concert. Then, we exited the building and entered his car at 2 a.m. I buckled my grey seatbelt around my hips. So, my dad drove off in the direction of Ottawa. We talked to each other for a bit. Then, I lay my head down on the headrest above my adult car seat, and my eyelids fell over my eyes. My eyelids remained enclosed for the rest of the trip. Then, he dropped me off at home at 6 a.m. I slept at my mom's two-bedroom apartment for a scanty period. Then, he picked me up and drove his car to my high school at 8 a.m. I entered the first classroom of my schedule on that day. I conducted myself identically to the way in which I would conduct myself, if I had slept for seven hours. I still achieved consciousness in classes, and I achieved focus on the teachings in all of my assigned classrooms on that day.

I came home two days in a row, crashing into the spongy mattress of my bed. I felt fatigued. So, I swiftly fell asleep. Then, I awoke and rose from my bed. I asked my mom to carry out my homework. *I do not have time to do it after sleeping in bed in the late afternoon until the evening*, I figured. Then, she executed my homework.

Moreover, I was having difficulty with getting to my first class of the day on time on different occasions. My alarm clock repeatedly neglected to go off at the time, for which I set it. So, as soon as I arrived in our well-lit classroom on one morning, my bespectacled teacher sent me to the office to grab a pink slip. This slip indicated that I was tardy for the English class.

On a couple of occasions, while I sat at my desk in a classroom at the high school, my neck involuntarily moved my head in a certain direction. Nevertheless, it was not triggered by hubbub.

My second episode of heart arrhythmia took place while I was in a classroom at the same high school. It came out of the blue, while my female teacher was instructing us. She had short, brown hair. She was our music instructor. I felt my heart palpitate, as I sat in the classroom at my desk. Other students were seated at their desks, as well. I did not manage to catch what she communicated. Nevertheless, I stayed in the classroom and the episode of heart arrhythmia subsided.

On one of the last occasions in which I was present at Canterbury High School, Alyssa and Carlos lingered in the locker room hallway with me. Alyssa was a teenager with blond, long hair, and Carlos was a boy with a buzzcut. No one else remained in the hallway. Alyssa approached me and pushed me up against a locker. She was groping my torso like a male would in a film. She vocalized a sentence in a libidinous manner.

"Carlos, help" I said, laughing. I pretended to be joking. Nevertheless, I felt really awkward about her actions and about requesting his help. I thought, *She'll get mad or offended if I show that I'm seriously petitioning for his aid.* He did not break her away from me. Then, they left the portion of the hallway in which I was located. When I thought that they were out of earshot, I screamed. My soul had been fragmented by that instance of homosexual harassment.

At home, I informed my mom of my decision to quit school. My decision stemmed from my physical health concerns. She accomplished all of the needed tasks relating to my departure from school. After I departed from school, I felt fatigue. So, I lay down in bed for much of the day. This occurred on the daily.

On one day, my mother handed me a thin book on different religions, which she bought for me. I scanned it. I came across Buddhism in there, Christianity and other religions. The ones that intrigued me the most were Christianity and Buddhism. I discovered that Buddhism believed in honesty and selflessness. It resembled Christianity and it held some of the same values as I held.

Then, on another day, my mom approached me.

"You are going to see a psychiatrist on Wednesday," my mom said out of the blue.

"Why?" I said. I do not remember the reason that she uttered. I felt devastated.

Since I was a teenager, I desired others to make decisions for me. I did not want to make decisions for myself. I sought to do what pleased others.

Then, I went to my bedroom and sat on a chair alone. I prayed to God, petitioning Him for a way out of this predicament. I had not prayed to God for months and had consciously given up on God. I had rendered myself my god. I was hoping that He would avert this appointment with a psychiatrist. Then, I felt the peace of God flood over me. "And the peace of God, which passeth all understanding, shall keep your hearts and minds through Christ Jesus" (Phillippians 4:7).

I approached her. Then, I expressed my desire to avoid a psychiatric appointment. Nevertheless, she was adamant about her decision to bring me to one.

On the following day, I spoke on the phone to my close friend, Natasha, about the peace that had come over me. She listed five other reasons as possibilities for the peace that I had experienced. She believed that one of them was the reason for the peace.

"No," I said. "That's not why."

"God does not exist," she said. During the conversation, I started to doubt that God existed. Later on after the phone conversation was over, I approached my mom.

"Does God exist?" I said.

"Yes," she said. "He exists."

"Oh," I said. "I'm so relieved to hear that!"

Psychiatrist

When the day came for my mom and I to meet the psychiatrist, we mounted a bus. Then, she pulled the yellow cord, when our bus was nearing the bus stop. Then, we dismounted the bus by descending the black steps. My mom led me to the building of the clinic. Then, we entered a spacious, and secluded room. A bespectacled man was sitting in his chair, and he greeted us. He had short, light-brown hair. He was the psychiatrist.

He conducted himself in a courteous manner. I told him that I had been experiencing panic attacks. Nevertheless, they were not panic attacks. That was merely what I had heard them named. They were episodes of heart arrhythmia. Then, he gave me an oral quiz.

"You have social anxiety," he said.

"I thought you would say that," I said. He prescribed a type of medication to me. It was named Lorazepam.

While I was outside, crossing the road from a bus stop, I did not distinguish a difference between when I ingested it, and when I did not ingest it. I felt joyful, but I was joyous before taking it, too.

I returned to his office, and informed him, that I would not be revisiting his room for another session.

"If you leave now, you'll never get better," he roared angrily, as I departed from the room. As I walked away, my back was facing him.

Some days afterwards, I spoke to my dad over the phone. I told him about my experience with the one tablet of this drug.

"It was a placebo," he said.

"My mom did not tell me so," I said.

When I told my mom what my dad had uttered, she denied that it was a placebo.

I suffered from involuntary movements in my legs at times at home. One of them would just move (while I was sitting on a chair) in an unforeseen direction. This type of movement was not transpiring, after I consumed the placebo. I had only taken the placebo once.

I went from doctor to doctor to try to discover what was ailing me. One doctor gave me a laboratory requisition form, which gave me leave to get my blood drawn at a laboratory. So, I went to the laboratory and I had it drawn with a needle. When the doctor reported the results from the bloodwork, he said that I had iron-deficiency anemia. My mom recommended that I go on a vegetarian diet. So, I switched to a vegetarian diet in order to overcome my anemia.

My mom told me that she had set me up with correspondence courses, because I had been dealing with episodes of arrhythmia. My episodes of arrhythmia sporadically occurred in the first set of episodes, but, eventually, they became continuous.

Dora came to my front door and I met her for the first time. She had black hair, and medium brown skin like Barack Obama. She brought a bible correspondence course pamphlet. It was the first lesson in the series. Once I finished that one, my mom mailed it. We received a grade and corrections on the answer sheet, and we received the next lesson in the course in the same envelope by mail. Through this course, I discovered that without a shadow of a doubt, Jesus was God. I discovered His divinity. Before then, I supposed that He was just a human, who had passed away on a cross. I had not perceived why humans had made a fuss over Him at my Catholic church.

I went through various bible courses, and I watched a lot of films from the colporteur, Dora. They were not fictitious. They were all founded on the belief that Jesus is our Saviour and Lord. One of the VHS tapes was intended for those, who intended to get baptized. I eagerly put the latter tape into the slot of my VCR. Then, I viewed the video, as it played on our TV screen. A pastor held the woman's hand, and he covered her mouth with a cloth. Then, he dunked her under the water. Then, he lifted her hand up from the water. Then, she came up out of the water right away, and the spectators clapped. This was an immersion, which I had not experienced as a spiritual rite. The only thing close to that kind of baptism, that I had experienced, was a sprinkling of water on me. A Catholic priest had performed it, when I had been a baby.

Every Saturday, Dora drove her minivan with my mother and I in tow to a nearby church. This continued for years until she subscribed to another denomination. Then, she ceased her rides for us to that church.

I viewed the film, *The Shining*, on my own at my home. When certain music came on (that was intended to instill fear in people), my heart beat started to race. So, I decided to stop the observation of this film by me. I did not watch the remainder of the film on that day. Moreover, I decided to refrain from the watching of horror films again.

"I want to get baptized," I told Dora. Dora rejoiced in that fact.

"I want to get baptized," my mom said to Dora. We were baptized a month afterwards along with other people. After the moment of my baptism, I felt like I was walking on cloud nine. I was 18 years of age. Some days after the fact, I told the chiropractor's wife about it, rejoicing. She was a tall Caucasian lady. She rejoiced over it with me.

Eventually, I switched to a vegan diet, so that I would improve my physical health.

At one point, I asked God to take my episodes of arrhythmia away. I asked that I no longer have them once more.

"Jump off a balcony and [have sex with] all of the boys," she said to me out of the blue. We were at home in the month of September. I omitted the swearword that she used. I do not desire that people see that term in this book. At that point in time, I was stunned. I did not reply to her word curse. "Don't tell anyone I said that." We had a balcony, that was high up on that apartment.

On one day in October, my father informed me, that my mom had lied to me. She had pretended to have signed me up for correspondence courses. She had fabricated the story, that the courses' materials were taking a long time to come to us by mail.

"She is worse than I thought," I said.

"I know," he said.

One day, I played the Ouija board solo at my dwelling. Nevertheless, that was the last time, that I employed it. A little while after my baptism, I informed my mom, that I wanted to throw the Ouija board of mine out. So, she permitted me to carry that out.

My dad handed me a book on writing. It was written by Julia Cameron. It was called, *The Vein Of Gold: A Journey to Your Creative Heart*. I discovered automatic writing through this book, and I began to practice it for the first time. I even practiced it each morning.

Eventually, I went to another high school full-time. During my studies there, I noticed, that I did not suffer from episodes of arrhythmia any longer. *God has healed me from them*, I realized. Then, I studied for some semesters, and, thus, I completed my high school studies.

I would hear a lot of shouting while residing with my mom and her boyfriend. Mostly, she was the one shouting at him, and he was not shouting in return. She was executing it out of anger. When these moments came, I would either cover my ears with my hands or I would cover them with a pair of noise-cancelling headphones.

Pugwash

I read a book from Ellen White, which was in digital format. She enumerated the effects of masturbation, and they were novel to me. This book convicted me. So, I ceased from masturbation at the age of 21.

I told my mom about the emotional abuse, that Luc was inflicting on me. So, I requested, that she converse with him about it. I desired, that she resolve the matter. Instead, she said, that she would not communicate with him about it. She did not stick up for me.

At one point, I moved to my dad's place. Nevertheless, he treated me in a scornful manner. He scornfully laughed at my actions at the brick-and-mortar store and at home. His eyes did not show the love that I was longing for. During my whole life, I had been longing for a home in which there would be love, acceptance, and affirmation. I did not come upon it yet. Then, I moved to a women's shelter. I discovered that the shelter was cold overnight. So, I resolved to vacate the women's shelter. All these relocations stemmed from the hurt that I had felt from the abuse at my mom's dwelling. Then, I moved to Aunt Denise's house. I lived, ate, and slept at her residence for two weeks. Then, she told me to depart from her home. She said, that she feared that a fire would take place from my cooking. Nevertheless, no fire had ever occurred at her place from my cooking. I left her place, and I resumed my residency at my mom's apartment.

I attended the University of Ottawa for some months. In one of the classes there, I met a teacher. He was quite good-looking and quite kind. He taught us the Advanced French class. It consisted of things that I had already learned in another class through a college. So, it was really easy.

The class was taught in French and, so, all the students spoke in French. The students were all around my age. This was an entrance class. It was assigned to so-called "special" students. This kind of students were the ones who had been accepted into their requested program yet.

While I sat in the classroom, I heard the teacher say: « Qui est Sandra? Qui est Sandra? Qui est Sandra? » He looked excited on the first day (in which I attended his class. It was January. The class was called Grammaire & Style.

« Bonjour !» he said in a European-French accent, months afterwards, while I was sitting on the blue, padded bench at outside of the classroom at Simard.

« Bonjour » I said, smiling. He was whistling, creating a melody. Then, we stood up and headed to his classroom.

I developed an infatuation with him. Nevertheless, he wore a wedding ring on his ring finger on his left hand. He was 32 years young and I was 25 years young.

At one point in time, while I was hanging out with a friend, I discovered that she did not wear bras. Then, I found a forum online that included females that claimed that they went braless in public. Now, I had not ever gone braless since I was 12 or 13 years young. My puberty began at 12 years of age. Nevertheless, I found bras uncomfortable sometimes. So, I ventured out in the braless movement. I ceased wearing a bra in public and even went braless to Mahmoud's class. Mahmoud was the professor of the French class that I was bringing up earlier.

A middle-aged man came over to our home to install the washer and dryer of mine. He conducted himself in a talkative manner towards me.

"You should get married," he said. Before then, I had been feeling content with singlehood. At that point in time, I was executing my studies at the University of Ottawa.

On one Saturday at church, a church member invited me to attend a camp meeting at Pugwash. Camp Pugwash was located in Nova Scotia. I concurred with him on this invitation. Moreover, I persuaded a female friend to join me on this trip. He brought a brown-haired, little girl with him on the train trip of ours. She appeared to be six and a half years of age. He was an elderly, married man with short, white hair.

At the camp meeting, people testified of meeting their spouse at Canadian University College. Nevertheless, this university was renamed Burman University during the latter part of my studies there. This camp meeting was geared towards believers in God and in Jesus. *God is speaking to me through these testimonials,* I thought. Nevertheless, I neither tested the spirits, nor perceived how to do so.

So, I went from one adventure to another. I moved to Burman University and commenced my studies there. It was located in Lacombe, Alberta. My program was music. I was admitted into the Bachelor's Degree in Music program. Nevertheless, I changed it to a Bachelor's Degree in Secondary Education with theology as a major and music as a minor. Eventually, I changed my Bachelor's Degree to Elementary Education. Lastly, I switched it to a Bachelor's Degree in General Studies. That was my program towards the end of my studies at BU.

An Encounter

One day, I joined Canada Youth Challenge towards the end of spring. A man drove me to a home in Calgary, Alberta. When I entered the place, I realized, that it needed to be prepared for occupancy. It did not have the electricity set up yet. Nevertheless, by the next day, the electricity was set up. Then, more group members joined us at the residency.

One day, I heard a doorbell ring. So, I opened the front door of our house, and a man grinned at me courteously. He had black, curly hair and white teeth. His skin was light brown. I greeted him. He stepped into the home. He treated me in an overly charming manner, as he spoke to me. *He is the kindest man that I have ever met*, I thought.

Lorkens spoke to me on the phone for the first time. At one point, I told him, that I desired to have a friendship before starting any amorous relationship. He said that he concurred with me. Nevertheless, his actions expressed otherwise. He asked to communicate with me through Skype two days in a row after that initial conversation on the phone. So, we did so. He claimed that he wanted to get more acquainted with me. He communicated with me in English in a somewhat poor manner.

CHAPTER 4

NAÏVETÉ

I lay in bed one night, feeling so cherished. The guy, that I liked, had just commenced an amorous relationship with me. I treasured him, but I was not well acquainted with him. This was turning into a long-distance relationship. I thought, *this is beneficial. One can avoid sexual temptation through a long-distance relationship. This relationship is adventurous. We are both from different countries, backgrounds, and even have a different skin colour. It resembles the relationship of forbidden love between Romeo and Juliet.*

Nevertheless, I was subconsciously desiring another guy. I had been asking him time after time to meet me in certain locations on campus on certain days, because I missed him terribly. Whenever an event (that I liked) turned up on campus, I invited him to it. Then, we met up at those locations. The teenager had black, curly hair. He was tall.

"Are you two in a relationship?" Ambra said, while him and I were at an outside gathering of people on one evening. Neither of us answered her query.

On another occasion, we met up at a lounging area with couches. I thought, *it resembles a romantic relationship, but our scheduled meet-ups have not amounted to any progress in that area. Moreover, he is under-age; he is 19 years young. I am 26 years young. So, I feel uncomfortable with the thought of a romantic relationship with him.* I never tried to kiss him nor something else similar to that.

During this second school year at Burman University, I suffered from a lot of desire. I was struggling with keeping it under wraps. I also did not know what the root of it was nor what I was thinking subconsciously. I just thought that lust was thinking that a man was handsome. I thought that it was harmless. I had been honestly falling in lust with different guys in Canada Youth Challenge and, then, at school. My search for the suitable guy as my husband was an obsession. *He has to fit a certain criteria*, I thought. *He has to be of the same denomination as me. I want him to be a good father to my future children. I do not want him to practice corporal punishment on my children.*

On the following day, I conversed with Lorkens and his cousin on Skype. His cousin had dark brown skin and curly, black hair. Zoom did not exist yet for the general public. Throughout the conversation, his cousin was repeatedly guffawing. It was not in a friendly manner; it was in a condescending manner.

On the next day, I discussed kissing with my boyfriend on Skype. I said that I neither wanted to French-kiss outside of marriage nor even kiss his cheek, etc. Then, he sneered. So, I broke off the relationship with him. I figured that if he did not respect these boundaries, the relationship would not be a productive one.

I went on Facebook and discovered photos of my ex-boyfriend with a broken-hearted, defeated expression on his face.

"Will you marry me?" he said in a typed message on Facebook in January of the following year. That message occurred months afterwards.

"No," I responded in a touch-typed message.

When the springtime came around, one of the members of Canada Youth Challenge invited me and others on Facebook to join Canada Youth Challenge for the upcoming "summer" program. *His invitation is unwelcome and suspicious*, I thought. *Nevertheless, I do not want to appear rude.* I believe that God was placing the desire in my heart to refuse this invitation. Nevertheless, I signed up for the second summer program of mine with Canada Youth Challenge. Canada Youth Challenge is a youth scholarship program, in which students offer materials on a donation basis. The materials contain Christian content and students go door-to-door, offering these materials.

Each year in which I participated in the Canada Youth Challenge program, our team members lived in the same home. We ate our meals at the same time. We showered at roughly the same time. Our leaders had a strict schedule which they followed. They ordered us to go to bed at the same time. They ordered us to head out on the road at the same time. We were like an army, except less strict.

We had a different partner on each outing of ours when doing our colporteur volunteering. We headed out on the field almost every day to execute it. We brought our walkie-talkies with us for emergencies. We also knew the codes for different types of emergencies.

During the summer program of CYC of that year, when I first met Lorkens, he did not greet me warmly. He looked hurt. So, I gave him a hug.

"Where are you from?" I said at another moment.

"Haiti," he said.

"Cool!" I said, but I had very limited knowledge about Haiti. During the program, we got along so well. He kept discussing a relationship with me, even though he was one of the leaders in the program in Alberta, Canada. *The rule in CYC is that no romantic relationships should take place during the program*, I thought. *So, I do not want a romantic relationship with him until after the program would end. The rule should be respected.* So, I expressed this desire to him.

I prayed to God about getting engaged to this fellow. I did not make out a response. So, I was unaware of what His will was regarding this matter.

Lorkens said that he had desired to marry someone who is underage. Nevertheless, God instructed him to wed me. I did not question these things; I did not bring these claims into a discussion with God. I took them as facts.

"Should I marry Lorkens?" I asked Kemar. He had short, black, curly hair. He often wore glasses.

"Yes," Kemar said. "Go for it."

On each time that the end of the Canada Youth Challenge program was approaching, I cried a lot. On the second summer of mine in a row in this program, this transpired on one morning. It was the last day of the satellite part of the program. "Satellite" is the name for the program when we go off as a partition of the whole to certain cities. It is a rigorous part of the program. It occurred after training.

In this moment, I was not managing to hold back my tears. We were in the sanctuary of a church and all of our team was seated in the pews. I felt my soul fragment from the thought of parting from my comrades soon. They had been with me through thick and thin. We had been like a team and a family.

On another day, our team and others arrived in a minivan at a huge park after the necessary part of the program had ended. Our team was the last to arrive in the morning there after working like workhorses. I was lying down on back seats in the minivan while two guys sat in another area of the minivan, talking in the front seats.

I exited the minivan and walked for a bit. Then, I spotted Lorkens and we started talking. We walked outdoors together.

"I would like to spend my life with you," Lorkens said. Then, we put on our life jackets and pushed the canoe off the shore. Then, we sat in the same canoe on a lake. It was only the two of us. I pondered the words that he had just expressed. Nevertheless, I did not query God about it on that day. The whole canoe ride seemed romantic and innocent. Nevertheless, I did not feel certain, that God desired, that I get engaged to Lorkens. Eventually, I gave him a yes. Then, we stood near each other with the rest of the Canada Youth Challenge under a big, black gazebo.

Throughout my engagement to Lorkens, he gave me many compliments. On the first day of our engagement, a guy walked up to us, while we were seated at a table. "I know what's going to happen. She's going to divorce you," he said. He pointed at me, and he gave a warning look to Lorkens. I thought, *Why is he looking at me in a manner so as to say, that I am evil and not to be trusted?*

"She will not," Lorkens said in a protective manner. I smiled.

Engagement

I returned to Ontario. During my dad's first encounter with Lorkens, Lorkens and I were seated on the couch side by side at my mom's apartment. He repeatedly lifted up my top a bit, and I kept pulling it down. After that meeting, my dad said something to the effect that this guy is not marriage or relationship material. I was in lust, and I did not heed his comment. *I am in love,* I thought. *My good influence will change Lorkens for the better, because he loves me.* He had not lifted up my top before then.

On one occasion, while Lorkens and I were seated on chairs at my mother's apartment, Luc was in the same room as us. Nevertheless, he was at the other end of the living room. Luc was eyeing me with a murderous look on his face. Lorkens emitted a disapproving sound from his mouth. Nevertheless, Lorkens did not say a thing. Luc did not give me that look again since then. He used to eye me in this manner from time to time. So, I figured that Lorkens must have spoken to him in private about this matter.

On another day, Lorkens and I were in my dad's vehicle. My dad stopped the car at a gas station, and he exited the car. Then,

Lorkens removed his seatbelt, and he came really close to me. His legs touched my knees. I was seated in the back seat of the car, as he executed this act.

In the beginning of our engagement, Lorkens and I spoke on the phone and he laughed if I laughed. He appeared to feel empathy. Moreover, we saw eye to eye.

On another occasion, he asserted that I did not look healthy. He sent photos to my email inbox of women who he found appeared healthy.

He instructed me to eat more food. This occurred during my semester at Burman University. He wanted me to gain weight, even though my weight (according to the doctors) was in the ideal range. They were judging by my BMI and having me weigh myself on a scale at the clinic. Nevertheless, I piled as much food as I could consume onto my tray at the cafeteria at Burman University. I weighed myself daily, but I only gained two pounds.

We had a long-distance relationship, but we communicated over our phones per diem. Toward the close of the engagement, I was talking for the greatest part of the period of each phone conversation of twenty minutes. During each conversation, he said nothing bordering on the whole time. This continued day after day.

"May we shorten the phone calls, since you don't talk? You don't seem interested in what I have to say," I said.

"No," he said. So, they continued to last twenty minutes. I cried after having a phone call with him. I felt unloved by him.

At one point, during my studies at university, Shynell was at my dormitory unit. Shynell possessed long, black hair and dark-brown skin and she possessed white teeth. She was fit. We were in the kitchen. The kitchen possessed a white-tiled floor. "I'm engaged!" I excitedly told her.

"Really?" she said. "To who?"

"To Lorkens," I said. "He's a guy I met through Canada Youth Challenge in Calgary."

"I didn't even hear that you were in a relationship," Shynell said. I was not intimate with her, but we talked to each other every so often. She treated me kindly, and I did the same to her. I really enjoyed conversing with her in general.

On another day, Shynell approached me.

"I'm concerned about this relationship that you have with this man," she said. "Please, don't go through with it. I care about you. That's why I'm saying this."

My university teacher spoke to me indoors on another occasion. She had short, dark, brown hair. "Why do you want to marry him?" Sara said. "You will have a bad relationship, if you do so. I'm warning you, because I care about you." I was a friend of hers. I had befriended her before I attended my first class of hers.

"Okay," I said. "You care about me. That's why you said this. I'm fine. My relationship is going well. It's the best one I've ever had actually." I really lacked transparency with people and I denied issues. I had little experience with healthy relationships. I tended to speak like everything was rosy in my life. I feared admitting that something was negative in my life.

On another occasion, I was in a taxi, and informed the driver of my engagement.

"A lot of immigrants are getting married in order to immigrate to Canada," he said. "I'm warning you. Be cautious!" *My fiancé is not planning any such thing*, I thought. So, I brushed it off. A year before the wedding date (which was in August of 2025), I started to feel unwell physically. I felt a little weakness and some fatigue, while I stayed at my mother's apartment. So, instead of returning to school in September of that year, as I had been planning, I headed back to school in January of the following year: 2015.

While Lorkens stayed at my dad's place during the Christmas break in 2014, Lorkens did not obey my principles regarding touch. He touched me more and more in inappropriate ways. He even did so when my dad entered the living room on one occasion.

"Look," I said, as my dad opened the door of the veranda. "My dad's here." Then, he exited the veranda, entering the living room, and slid the door shut. I felt uncomfortable. I did not want my dad to see Lorkens touching my clothing in the area covering my breasts.

Then, after I returned to Burman University, I suffered from the flu. So, I informed my fiancé about it. He recommended that I consume some lemon juice. So, I took some lemons and squeezed juice out of one. I mixed lemon juice with some water day after day. It did reduce the flu symptoms. Nevertheless, the flu lasted a month. Therefore, I looked up witchcraft on the

Internet to see if peradventure that was bringing me to feel ill before my marriage to Lorkens.

I purposed to volunteer at a gym in a nearby school. Lorkens asked me what I would wear. I acquainted him with the plan of mine to wear a skirt.

"I don't want you to wear a skirt at a gymnasium," Lorkens said. "I don't want you to wear a skirt when playing sports. People call it unsociable. You should consider this subject. You are a woman, so you will react to it. Women emotionally react to things."

I attended a church on King Edward Avenue for the first time, while I was dwelling in Ottawa, Ontario. It was a francophone church. A man was leading the Sabbath school instructing in a certain area and other leaders did the same thing in other spots. I was seated in a pew, looking up at him as he taught us. The teacher was very nearby.

"You women don't know how bad you are until you get married," he said.

On another occasion, while I spent time at my mom's place, Étienne and Lorkens were present. Étienne had short, dark-brown hair. Étienne was conducting a bible study.

"Why do you want to marry her if you have nothing in common?" Étienne said, eyeing Lorkens.

"She dresses modestly and she is Adventist," he said.

On another occasion, Lorkens and I were holding a private conversation.

"We will get up at 5:30 in the morning together," Lorkens said. "When we'll be married, we'll go out for walks together every day." I had been arising at 5:30 each morning for many months. It had been effortless for me. So, I looked forward to executing these activities with him.

About six months before our wedding day, Lorkens asked me how many children I wanted. I said that I desired to have three to five children. I wanted a big family in order to make up for what I had not experienced as an only child.

CHAPTER 5

MARRIAGE

I spent my wedding day, preparing my body for my wedding night. This preparation used up two hours. I was prepared to depart quite early and Uncle Gérald came over to our apartment. Uncle Gérald was a tall man with tanned skin. He was muscular. I was waiting for the driver to arrive at my home, and I did not want to be late. So, I asked Uncle Gérald to drive me there. *I want to arrive there early*, I thought. He agreed and he drove me to the church. I went through the parking lot, and Uncle Pierre eyed me, smiling. Uncle Pierre had short, brown hair. He was tall. We greeted each other. I was wearing my regular clothes. He entered the building about ten steps ahead of me. Then, I entered the church building, and put on my white wedding gown. I styled my hair in the way that my husband had said that he liked.

"Does it look good?" I asked my two bridesmaids.

"No," they said. Then, the other bridesmaid showed up. Her name was Katrina. Katrina was wearing high heels. She had black hair and pale skin. She had Chinese blood in her.

"Does my hairdo look good?" I said.

"Yes," Katrina said. She pulled up the zipper at the back of my wedding dress. She held it firmly up to the point that I felt the heel of my feet lift off of the floor a bit.

"Thank you," I said. A little afterwards, Lorkens was coming into the basement of the church, which was where I was located. I concealed myself behind a door.

My bridesmaids left me one by one. I told my maid of honour to come back to me. I told her to inform me when it would be my turn to stroll down the aisle. A half hour later, the pastor approached me in the basement.

"We've been waiting for you," he said. "You're half an hour late."

"No," I said. "I've been here. I arrived early. I told Katrina to tell me, when it's time to go up." Then, I notified the pastor that I will mount the staircase. So, he departed from the basement, as he mounted the staircase. I went up the stairs, holding up the front part of my white dress. My dad was sitting on his black walker seat outside of the sanctuary with a smile on his face. The smile looked calm.

Call it off, God said. It sounded like a thought of mine. Moreover, I did not recognize His voice.

I do not want my dad to feel anger, I thought. *He has spent so much money on this wedding.*

I came over to my dad and greeted him. Then, a man put my dad's brown dress shoes on his feet. The second brown dress shoe fell apart.

"What!" my dad said with guilt on his face as he strolled with me down the aisle. A classical melody played as we entered the sanctuary. I wore sympathy and guilt on my face. When I first laid my eyes on my husband (while he was in the sanctuary on that day), he was speaking to his best man right near his ear as he eyed me with a suspicious look. The guests in the pews stood up and music played as we strolled down the aisle. The guests eyed me in wonder. I was wearing a dress that touched the floor. It covered my legs, and my torso. The sleeves were really short, but I wore a little white, tight shirt underneath it. I was wearing flat, white dress shoes.

My father left me and entered a pew while Lorkens took his place in the aisle. Then, I took Lorkens' arm and we walked down the rest of the aisle. The pastor was standing at the front of the aisle.

We read our wedding vows. Then, when all was said and done, I watched for Lorkens to initiate the first wedding kiss, as is tradition in Canada. It did not occur. So, I initiated it. The audience applauded.

After The Wedding Day

We experienced our honeymoon in Québec for some days. We did not pay the rent for our stay at the hotel, because my dad was covering the cost of it. Then, we relocated to a woman's house in Ottawa, Ontario. For the first two weeks of our marriage, Lorkens was strolling outside with me daily. Then, he determined that he did not desire to do that daily. After a little while, he stopped walking with me altogether outside for months. Moreover, around that time, while we were still living at the woman's place, he ceased daily quality time with me.

Nevertheless, he was spending quality time each night with the Haitian woman, who took us in. She was a lady in her 40s or 50s. She had light brown skin. While I was in bed, my husband washed the dishes at 10:00 p.m. It was dark outside. Then, he chatted with the woman. I could hear them conversing, while I waited, lying in bed, for my husband to join me. They got along well.

There were times when a light was left on in the basement and the woman roared angrily at me (from the main floor) to extinguish it. *I do not know how she knows that it is on,* I thought. *The winding staircase and the wall should have hidden that fact. Usually, if not every time, my husband is the one who leaves it on.* I tended to shut off lights before exiting a room. My mom had taught me to do so from childhood. Nevertheless, he did not have this habit.

My husband left a light on on the main floor, while we were in her presence. The woman did not angrily roar at him for it, and she did not even correct him for it. This was favouritism. My husband paid for the groceries. On the last day in which I lived there, the woman brought up the fact that a banana had gone in a bin, in which she did not want it to go. (I had put it in there, after my husband stated that it was the bin for produce. If that were true, then, I had been putting the produce in the wrong bin all along.) She said this in the presence of my husband, while we all were seated in her living room. "I thought that that was where you wanted it to go," I said. "Why are you criticizing me on it now?"

"So you'll know," she said. On the following morning, we departed from her house. We had dwelt there for a month. Then, we headed off by plane to Lacombe, Alberta.

About six months into the marriage, I realized some new things. *I made a mistake in marrying Lorkens*, I thought. *I could not blame anyone else for it. It is my fault. I want to divorce him, because he does not love me.* So, I informed a male friend about it. Nevertheless, my friend said that people would look down on me for divorcing him so soon. So, I continued to stick it out, even though my soul was fragmenting. *The thing is that it resembles a nightmare*, I thought. *Nevertheless, in a nightmare, you wake up from it in the morning. When you are in a marriage, you go through it day by day, week after week, and month after month. You don't simply wake up from it. It goes on for a long time.*

Graduation

On the day preceding my graduation, a male friend of mine approached me. I was in the dorm hallway, just exiting my little home in the basement. I was in the process of shutting the front door. The hallway floor was covered in a very long rug. It went from one end of the hallway all the way to the end of the hallway.

"Hey, Tyrone," I said. Tyrone had light brown skin and short, curly hair. He was tall.

"Hey, Sandra," he said. "I wanted to let you know, I will be attending the grad, but I won't be showing up to see you. I'll be showing up to see my friends." I felt quite displeased, but I tried to conceal it. *He does not care about me*, I thought.

"Okay," I said. I said "okay" in response to things in general, even if I did not concur with them. *He is saying that because we are in front of Lorkens' place*, I thought. *Or, maybe, he does not desire to offend me. I had told him to refrain from flirting with me.*

On the following morning, I donned a black, long gown and a black mortarboard hat. The gown flowed from my shoulders. I exited the bathroom in the Admin building. It was a big, white building, where secretaries were present. Then, I exited that building and walked down the footpath right up to the one that was two buildings away from it. Then, I entered the brown church building and approached a lineup of people. We watched for our next cue, as other students entered the sanctuary. Then, the period of time came for our turn. So, we strolled down the lit aisle in the sanctuary. There were pews on either side of it. Then, we took our seat in a pew. When my name was called, I went up the stairs and onto the stage. The president of the school was onstage. He had straight, jet black hair and pale skin. He was tall and bespectacled. I approached him, and I grinned at him. He shook my hand. Then, he handed me a scroll and some gifts, which I grasped. The scroll was rolled up and tied with a red ribbon.

"Thank you," I said. I was six months pregnant. So, my belly resembled a balloon. It was curved in a beautifully pregnant manner. A photo was taken of us as we turned to face the camera. We grinned, and I walked off of the stage. At one point, we all walked out of the building in a line. There was a flying drone overhead. It was the month of May. So, the weather was warm and the grounds were sunlit. Then, I came to the graduation party area outside. It was in front of the white Admin building. I watched for my husband and Lizzie to turn up. I had not spotted my husband during the ceremony. Lizzie appeared close to me within about five minutes. She had long, dark brown hair and pale skin. We greeted each other and struck up a conversation. *I do not feel satisfied,* I thought. *I want my husband to show up.* He popped up about 25 minutes after Lizzie approached me.

Did you attend the graduation ceremony?" I asked him.

"Part of it," he said.

"Did you see me onstage?" I said.

"I missed that," he said. "I came in afterwards." I had told him the time when the

graduation ceremony would start before my departure from our home on that morning.

"I saw it," Lizzie said.

"I caught Gimps graduating," he said. Gimps was our male friend. I felt heartbroken.

Then, we went to the photoshoot spot on the grassy knoll and got photos captured of us. The photos showed me with a heartbroken expression on my face. What Lorkens neglected to catch broke my heart.

As I went down the stairs from the outside area in front of the building, I came across

Kimmy. She had been my roommate in school. She possessed dark brown hair and pale skin. She was tall. Nevertheless, I did not have anything substantial to say to her. I felt like I had no enthusiasm to offer her. Since I had not spotted her in a long time, I should have had some enthusiasm.

I stepped down the staircase, which was on a little hill. Then, Tyrone took me in his arms all of a sudden.

Lorkens

My husband continually criticized my actions.

When I would request him to spend time with me, he would say, "I'm busy."

There came a point in the marriage, where when I would talk to him during our marriage, he would react in an angry manner on almost every occasion while we were at home (when the children and I were the only ones at home). This began while we lived in Québec. In public, he did not execute that for the most part. He put on a figurative mask for others (who did not live with us) to conceal how his behaviour really was with his household.

While I was at home, he conveyed that my habits were weird. He spoke to me as though my beliefs were mad.

After people would visit our home in Alberta, he would speak as if he was ashamed of what I had carried out or did not carry out during the visit. He would complain about the lack of cleanliness, etc. of our home.

Before I got married to Lorkens, he often caressed me. He caressed my top in the abdomen area or grasped my hand, for example. After I got married to Lorkens, when I moved in to hold him in my arms in the kitchen (or another place outside of our bedroom) after years of our marriage, he customarily pushed my arms away.

He would aim to make me compromise my values during my marriage and before our marriage. He would impose his view as the only option for me to take. He would portray his opinions as superior to mine and the standard, by which I and others should live by. So, I kept conceding my values and habits for what Lorkens said I ought to do. He kept saying that people did not carry out things the way in which I performed them. He neither respected my values nor my boundaries. He took the side of others and rejected mine. At home, his viewpoints were the only ones that he accepted (when no guest was over), and he hated individuality.

While I was pregnant with Soraya, my husband advised me to wear a bra. So, I began wearing one once more. Since then, I wore bras in public.

On one day, my daughter, Soraya, was sitting in her Baby Einstein activity jumper. She was only five months young. I was sitting on a chair nearby. Soraya was in my view. My husband left the dining room and entered his bedroom, shutting the door behind him. Then, my son swiftly turned the Baby Einstein activity jumper upside down. I screamed and stayed still. I was in shock. Then, my husband immediately exited the bedroom.

"My son flipped the activity jumper upside down with Soraya in it," I told him. Then, he put the activity jumper right side up. He took Junior to the bedroom and punished him for this act. Soraya did not have a single injury from that event.

On one day, I was in the kitchen in Edmonton, Alberta, and I spotted a photo of a naked woman on his cell phone screen. His cell phone was lying on the counter. Then, I heard the phone ring. He picked up the cell phone and walked out of the kitchen. He lifted the phone to his ear, grinning, as he stepped into the bathroom. Then, he entered my son's bedroom and he shut the door. After he exited the bedroom, I questioned Lorkens about the photo. He claimed that there had been no such photo on his cell phone.

On a Saturday afternoon, while my husband, the children and I were in his beigish, pink 90s Toyota Corolla sedan, the flashing sign for the train came on. It looked like my husband just wanted to ignore it and go through. That is illegal in Canada. He was driving the car up to the railroad track, while there was snow on the road. The car passed onto the railroad track, and it remained there. The train was approaching the car from the left, while my husband was in the seat on the left side of the car. The crossing gate came down on the hood of the car. Then, all of a sudden, he backed the car up in time to avoid a car accident from the train.

Seven days afterwards, it was a Saturday once more. My husband was in the driver's seat, and there was some ice on the road. We began to head out to church in his car on that morning. The road was sunny. He turned the steering wheel to the left. The car moved very little out of the dotted lane on the street. Then, he sharply turned the steering wheel to the right, while we were on a side street. So, the car veered to the right, and hit a truck. The truck was parked on the side of the road. It was an average-sized, white truck. I was in the front passenger seat on the right side of the car. I was right beside the area of damage to the car, but I did not sustain an injury.

"Is anyone injured?" I said, once the car was parked. I eyed my children. "Soraya, are you okay?"

"Yes," she said.

"Junior, are you okay?" I said.

"Yes," Junior said.

Born Again

During the year of 2020, I perceived that I was born again, though I did not get baptized in that year. I felt a trust in God that I had not experienced before then. I had great faith in God, and, in 2021, I became passionate about God. Moreover, I was unashamed of Him.

I attended my home church, which I had not attended in a long time. I had ceased attending it because I had been residing in another province in Canada. Then, when I came back for the first time, some people treated me differently. Some of them did not welcome me warmly. Some (who I was familiar with) acted like they did not know me. Moreover, they did not show me warmth when I spoke to them. They showed indifference. I wondered why their warmth had turned to indifference since I had left the church in 2015.

On the other hand, some people showed me warmth when I met them. One woman said that she loved me. The other woman was Gloria. She excitedly greeted me at the church. I sat with her in a brown pew and conversed with her. My children and my husband presented themselves at the church, too.

I greeted the pastor and he made a signal from a great distance away. He gave me a look, staring at me, like he was physically attracted to me. Nevertheless, he neither greeted me nor conversed with me. He acted like he did not hear me, when I greeted him. He was conversing with others at the church in the stairwell.

On the second time in which I attended the church, I said, "Hello" again to him. His name was Didier. Instead of greeting me, he called me selfish. I was constantly looking after my children and accompanying them during both visits at the church.

I greeted his son but his son did not say a thing. He appeared to be stunned by my greeting. He opened his mouth, but he did not manage to utter a thing. Nevertheless, he desired to voice something. He appeared to be 12 years of age and he possessed short, dark-brown hair.

Nevertheless, my husband did permit me to breastfeed Eve while he looked after the other two children in church. So, I executed that.

Then, after a visit at another church, the pandemic restrictions forbade us from the attendance of church gatherings. Moreover, churches ceased their church services.

In 2020, I discovered self-deliverance, and I performed it for the first time. God introduced me to the concept of demons through a video on YouTube in 2020. So, I did research on the matter.

Then, I discovered many more things on deliverance and demons. I learned that the Holy Bible supported it. I discovered new things about the stories that I had previously read about Jesus. I reread the stories of deliverance from blindness and other physical ailments, from which people had been suffering. He even delivered a boy from epilepsy. I had known that He had healed people from these things previously. Nevertheless, I had not known before then that physical ailments and/or physical issues were brought about by demons. In order to free those people from those ailments, Jesus had to deliver them from those demons.

God also taught me in 2020 through a certain person on You Tube, that God speaks to us nowadays. I used to believe that God only spoke to certain people: those who wrote the Bible; Ellen White; and those who spoke to Jesus, while He lived a human life on this Earth in the physical realm.

All the while, God was opening up my eyes to certain evil actions that people were doing in my life. He revealed what narcissism looked like, according to the DSM-5. This was a manual for psychiatry. God was exposing narcissism to me in detail. One person in my life (who had all the indicators of narcissism) was someone, who I had been closest to at one point.

God was instructing me to divorce my husband. Therefore, I viewed some videos on how to apply for a divorce in Ontario (while my baby was sleeping). I called my financial institution, and I requested a separate bank account for myself. So, the representative set that up for me. I even notified my husband that I purposed to get a divorce from him.

He verbally opposed it, as we discussed it. He was trying to convince me to cancel my plan. Moreover, I neither knew: how I would manage my chores; nor how I would take care of all of my three children at that point without his help. Nevertheless, at that time, I was doing all of those things mostly without his help. On the other hand, he was bringing in the money and working at a workplace outside of the home during the pandemic. I was still breastfeeding my baby once in the night. I was not receiving an income for a thing that I was doing. It was all free care for my children. It took up almost all of my time. So, I ceased from seeking a divorce from him, and ceased from moving in that direction.

~-----~

Two days after our nuclear family moved into our condo unit in Gatineau, Québec, my husband said that he had received an email from management. It was concerning a complaint from the neighbour, who lived below us.

Some days afterwards, he was knocking forcefully on the window of Soraya's bedroom. On another day, he was knocking hard on Eve's bedroom window, while she was quietly sleeping. Then, she woke up from the noise, and she was crying. Then, he repeatedly knocked on Soraya's bedroom window. He knocked on it so loud to the extent that I believed that her window would break, as I lay down in my bed. So, I rose from my bed, and walked to Soraya's bedroom. I did not see him, but I heard loud knocking. He was astral projecting to the window, which I did not realize at the time.

A week afterwards, my neighbour was swearing at my children while their bedroom window was open. My children and I were in Soraya's bedroom. So, I rebuked that.

Lorkens bought a thick, long, grey rug that covered almost the whole floor in the living room. Lorkens executed that in order to prevent loud noises. He desired to appease the neighbour. As the children played, they jumped and whatnot at times. They ran, too, at times, indoors. My husband also put a mat beside Lorkens Junior's bed for Lorkens Junior to land on when he would descend from his bed in the morning. He also put one beside our bed and beside Soraya's bed. I aimed to prevent noise in the place from our children, because I did not desire that the noise disturb the male neighbour.

My baby was sleeping and she was not making noise. Her name was Eve. She had dark brown hair and light brown skin. Neither my other children nor my husband were at home. They had left at about 9:29 a.m. I was just sitting at the computer, drinking some water quietly while listening to some quiet music. The pounding began about half of an hour after their departure. It appeared to arise from our neighbour's condo unit under our children's bedroom at our home. Our bedrooms were all on the same floor, and all of our other rooms were on the same floor. We did not have another floor nor a basement for our condo unit. The pounding appeared to be coming from this man's wall. On a separate occasion, the neighbour came to our front door, and I opened the front door. He possessed red hair and pale skin. He was tall. He was complaining about the noise. This transpired while my children and I were in the corner of the living room. The rug covered this area, and the rug was fat like a carpet. He appeared to be enraged.

Then, on another day, in the evening, I heard pounding coming from our front door. Lorkens confidently walked toward the front door, as I fled to my bedroom. I shut the bedroom door. Then, he opened the front door. I heard them conversing with one another, and, then, the neighbour departed.

While I raised my children, there was a small period of time in which Soraya and Junior obeyed my commands. Nevertheless, later on in their life, they started to behave in a disobedient manner towards me. Then, that became the frequent behaviour of theirs. Nevertheless, they did follow a schedule that I set out for them. I managed their mealtimes, snack times, playtimes, sleep times and resting times, according to the schedule. Therefore, I could work my socialization times into my days or evenings, even though I was their caregiver overtime. My work consisted of monitoring them and meeting their needs.

In December of 2020, my son stated that Eve was standing. I had not noticed, because I was preoccupied with other matters.

Then, I fixed my gaze on her and saw her standing inside her crib. She was holding on to a bedpost, while remaining in this position. That was the first time that I had spotted her standing. I was excited about her new skill. She was roughly seven months of age.

While Lorkens and I lived in Québec, Lorkens developed worse habits than previously in our marriage. When I would pose a query (such as "How are you?") to him, he would snap back at me.

While I lived in Québec (from the end of 2020 up to October of 2021), I almost never went outdoors except to exercise. I was grateful that my husband had a minivan. So, he did the shopping. My dad and my mom brought over groceries and other things from time to time. My dad customarily did so every two weeks, except for a little while when cross-border visitations (from Ontario to Québec) were forbidden. This was a restriction during the COVID-19 pandemic in which a great amount of people suffered from a lot of fear and fear-mongering.

I went out for walks in the evening. That was when my children were in bed or nearly in bed. My husband was at home, while I did so. Once when I was outside at around nine o'clock in the evening, rain started to pelt during my walk on my way home. I was neither donning a coat nor was I donning a jacket. A bucketful of rain pelted about half a meter from me, but it did not touch me. This occurred when I was near a certain, brown house. The house was made of brick.

While I lived with our family in Quebec, I headed to bed between midnight and 2 a.m. That was my bedtime. I slept in a bed. Then, I rose from my bed at 6:30 a.m. to feed Eve.

My husband had been ordering me time and time again to make the children refrain from shouting while he was working at home. Then, some days later, he asked me to have them not make any noise while he worked for eight hours a day in our bedroom at home. His rules became stricter and stricter. He claimed that he needed this quiet for the sake of his job.

In February of 2021, my husband informed me that he did not desire to sleep in the same bed as I. Moreover, he forbade me to sleep with him.

So, I slept on the couch night after night. On many nights in a row, when I lay down on the couch in the living room at bedtime, for the first 15 minutes, after initially shutting my eyes for a second, my eyes reopened and stayed open. They were scanning the home. I feared that someone would come in the front door and kill me at night. Those horror films from my childhood had really instilled fear in me. Nevertheless, my eyes used to not open once I shut them at bedtime. Moreover, they had not ever done so in order to scan my room for fifteen minutes.

My mother came over to our place each week and she spoke to us in a friendly manner. During most of the time which she spent at our condo unit, She was preparing food for the children and I.

I took care of the children and put them to bed in the afternoon. "Alright!" I said. "I'm going to take a rest."

"No," Lorkens said. "Don't rest. Stay up."

"Go, rest, Sandra," my mom said. Then, I immediately headed down the hallway and I entered my bedroom. I lay down in my bed.

On one day, I took the course, Fight Witchcraft and Win on the website of Breaking Curses 101. After completing the course, my eyes no longer scanned my bedroom for fifteen minutes after my bedtime. God had delivered me from this negative cycle. When I intended to sleep, I managed to keep my eyes shut after settling down on the purple couch at night.

In 2021, Lorkens had me attend lectures in our bedroom every two weeks. He was the lecturer. He lectured me on different, mundane things that I did. These lectures were not academic lectures. They were a form of scolding that he heaped on me. During this year, my heart was hardening from all of the emotional abuse that was heaped on me by my husband. Therefore, I was behaving in a harsh manner at times towards my children.

On one evening in our bedroom, he said that he believed that Christians could be

possessed by demons. I told him that Christians could be demonized, but not possessed by demons. He said that one man got baptized, then, was possessed by a demon in Haiti.

"Why did God order the Israelites to kill other people groups"? I had asked him about a year before then.

"It was because the other people groups were demons," Lorkens had said. *"They weren't humans."*

I took courses that brought me more deliverance and insight on deliverance and how to have a close walk with God.

On one day, when my iPad was on and the screen was facing me, I was taking one of these online courses for the first time. Lorkens came through the hallway from behind me.

"Oh, no," he said in a negative tone of voice. I turned my neck, and I spotted him. He was standing behind me, and he was staring at my screen. He sounded like he was suffering from fear.

My mother told me that she desired that I call the pastor of my former home church. My mother was not attending this church since many years ago. So, she had never met him. On another day, Gloria commanded me to call him. Gloria was an acquaintance of mine who was attending the church. This church had been the one that I had attended while living in Ottawa, Ontario. Nevertheless, I did not know the new pastor there. I concluded that I ought to acquire his phone number. After I retrieved it, I dialed his number.

He politely said, "Hello," which he had not done in church when I had met him in-person. Then, he was asking a question about what I understood about spiritual warfare. I was teaching him about that topic. He was unfamiliar with it. I felt that he was unfit to be a pastor because of his ignorance of that topic. Then, he went on his rant about what I was doing in my private life. I had not told him any of the things for which he was rebuking me. Apparently, someone had gossiped to him about me and he was rebuking me for living my life as a born-again believer in Jesus.

I did not pay attention to all that he was saying. I found that it was not inspired by God. It was an attack from the enemy. So, I kept the receiver away from my ears. It was a cordless phone. He was rebuking me for going for deliverance and taking courses on the Breaking Curses website.

During one evening, I spoke to Gloria on the phone. She was an acquaintance of mine from the church in Ottawa. I asked her about how to apply for governmental financial aid when one is going through a divorce (and when two spouses separate from each other). I asked her for a link regarding this matter.

She spoke to me about this matter, but she did not provide me with a link. She claimed that our friend, Sister Sohn and her would be arriving at our place. She was purposing to have a counselling session there for us. I informed her that I did not desire that.

Nevertheless, they showed up at our front door on one weekend. The children, my husband, my mom and I were present at home. They spoke to us in a friendly manner in our living room. Then, they entered a secluded room with my husband. Then, they came out and invited me into a group discussion with my husband.

I requested if I may talk to them in a secluded room before joining my husband. Nevertheless, they declined my request. So, I entered Lorkens Junior's bedroom while my mother was supervising the children. That is where my husband was present. They discussed the behaviour of mine. They condemned my behaviour, but spoke favourably of my husband's behaviour.

Then, they returned to our home for the second time. On this occasion, I wanted to be ready. I brought a sheet of lined paper with a list of negative behaviour that was exhibited by my husband. Then, I placed the sheet of paper on a beige dresser. I did not list those traits. Nevertheless, when I spoke to Sister Sohn, she did not make eye contact with my eyes. She looked down, ignoring what I was saying. At one point, she shouted at me in anger. She was blaming me for the fact that my husband was seeking a divorce from me. Then, I knew that this counselling was not aiding a thing. So, I headed to the bedroom door.

Gloria grabbed my wrist and locked the door.

"Don't leave," Gloria said. She stood in front of the door, blocking the way.

"Let me out of here," I yelled. I knocked on the door. Then, I pulled her hand off of my wrist. She moved out of the way and I unlocked the door.

I headed to the washroom and I prayed to God. My Bible was on my lap. I petitioned God to reveal to me a scripture to speak to me. He did so. I opened the bible and my eyes settled upon the scripture, Proverbs 14:7. I had neither known the number of the chapter for that verse nor the number of the verse by heart. It said:

"Go from the presence of a foolish man, when thou perceivest not in him the lips of knowledge" (Proverbs 14.7, KJV).

My mom came into the washroom, bringing me a toilet roll stand.

"Your dad's here," she said. I swiftly and excitedly left the washroom. Then, I spotted my father between the kitchen and the dining room. I ran up to him and gave him a hug, crying. I was so relieved to meet him.

"What happened?" he said. "Some kind of trauma." Then, I recounted the story to him. Then, we sat on the grey sectional couch and my mom joined us there. My father gave me empathetic looks of indignation as I told him more of the story.

"Ape," he said.

In June of that year, four policemen showed up at the front door of our condo unit. I let them into our home. My husband and my children were at home. I wore my baby carrier, which encapsulated Eve. She was facing me at the front of my torso. A policeman approached me.

« Votre mari nous a appelé en ce qui concerne votre santé mentale, » the policeman said. *Your husband called us concerning your mental health.* Three policemen formed a half-circle in front of me.

« Est-ce que vous voyez trois policiers ou trois démons? » another policeman said. *Do you see three policemen or three demons?*

« Je vois trois policiers, » I said. *I see three policemen.*

A female psychiatrist came to our place at the end of the visit.

« Es-tu déprimée? » she said. *Are you depressed?*

« Non, » I said. *No.*

« As-tu jamais tenté le suicide? » she said. *Have you ever attempted to commit suicide?*

« Non, » I said. *No.* Then, she asked me some other questions.

« Si tu as jamais besoin de l'aide, voici le numéro que tu peux appeler, » she said. *If you ever need some help, here is the number that you may call.* She handed me a card and she exited our home. Then, the medical respondant to emergencies said that I may call that number in case of a mental health emergency. Then, all of them departed.

My son was eyeing me four times a day in a murderous manner.

Therefore, I sought deliverance from Jesus through a recording of a course of mine online. I did the procedure, which included a recording on behalf of my son. From then onward, I did not see him give me that look again.

On the day of my husband and I's anniversary, I requested of him that we go out somewhere together. That did not transpire on that day. Nevertheless, two days afterwards, he took our three children and I into the minivan. He neither placed the seat (that was tucked under the floor of the Dodge Grand Caravan minivan) back in place, nor did he put both children (Lorkens, Junior, and Soraya) in separate booster seats. Instead, he placed them on the same adult car seat. Nevertheless, Soraya's booster seat was reaching past the edge of their (Junior and Soraya's) seat (which was the one under their booster seats. It was the kind of seat which adults sit on without a booster seat.

"Look," I said. "The children need to be in separate seats." He took off recklessly driving the minivan. He was speeding. Soraya was holding her small booster seat tightly (that did not have a back to it nor did her brother's) down with her hands as she moved in her seat. Both of their seats lacked a back to it. She looked like she was barely staying in her car seat, trying hard to not fall off onto the floor by pushing down on the sides of her booster seat. She aimed to keep the booster seat from moving off of her (adult) car seat. My son's booster seat was right beside the door of the minivan. My husband tore down the backstreet where there were condo units. Reckless driving was illegal.

He parked the minivan on black cement beside a water park. Then, we exited the minivan. The children were savouring their time at the splash pad and playing with the water that was spraying out of different points. I accompanied Eve and held her hand as she walked outdoors. I was wearing a baby blue skirt and it complemented my stomach. Their dad was near the children, as well. Moreover, other parents were present with their children at this water park.

Then, my husband and I sat at a table and a woman sat at the same table. My husband whispered something to the woman. I did not make out what he communicated.

« Qu'est-ce que tu vas avoir? » the woman said. *What will you be having?*

« Rien, » I said. « Je ne suis pas enceinte. » *Nothing. I am not pregnant.* I thought, *He must have told her quietly that I am pregnant. That is a lie. I am not pregnant.*

« Mais— » the lady said. *But—*

Then, we departed from the park and headed homeward in the minivan. Once we exited the minivan, a man appeared.

« Bonjour! » he said. *Hello!*

« Bonjour! » I said. *Hello!* Then, he handed me a document and I eyed it. It was entitled, « Demande En Divorce. » *Divorce Proposal*. I glared at the man.

« Bonne journée! » he said. *Have a nice day!* Then, he disappeared. I never spotted him before then nor since then.

CHAPTER 6

DIVORCE

When I read the divorce document, I discovered that it was signed by a criminal lawyer. His name was Paul. The list of statements that he said about me included one on the YouTube channel, from which I discovered the existence of demons. In the document the very thing that Lorkens told me to perform was what his lawyer was accusing me of doing.

The lawyer falsely accused me of not taking care of the children and leaving that to my husband. He false accused me of not being physically well enough to look after the children. The lawyer claimed that I was not sleeping in the same bed as my husband. He claimed that it was because I thought that he was demonized.

In court, my husband claimed that I was lying down often. He claimed that I did not have the energy to look after our children.

Some weeks afterwards, there were different court room sessions online that I attended. During one of them, one of my children was attending pre-school outside of our home and the other one was attending kindergarten at a public school. Eve was at home and she was a little over a year old. I was present at home, as well.

I addressed the divorce court judge with a smile. She had red, chin-length hair. I stated that I would prefer to talk to her in English. She liked me. Then, she spoke to me in English afterwards instead of in French. She questioned me, and I replied to her queries. My husband did not respond to a single question from the judge; only his criminal lawyer was responding to them on his behalf.

« Appelez le DPJ, » the judge said. *Call the DYP*. Then, she fixed her eyes on my eyes with a guilt-ridden expression. Est-ce que vous êtes d'accord de laisser le DPJ faire des rapports psychosociaux chez vous sur vous deux? *Are you okay with the DYP doing psychosocial reports at your home on the two of you?*

« Oui, » I said. *Yes*.

My mom, my husband's lawyer, and my husband were reporting my private life to one judge or another: even down to an email that I had sent to a friend of mine. Nevertheless, I had not sent this email to my husband.

"God is the One who is doing this," my close friend texted me. Her name was Nicole. She possessed blond hair, blue eyes, and pale skin. "It seems like the enemy is doing it, but God is causing this divorce to happen."

When my mother was over at our condo unit on one occasion, I sat with her on my husband's grey sectional couch.

"Would you, please, be a witness for me in this divorce court case?" I said, making eye contact with her. She possessed long, dark red hair at that point.

"I'm already going to be a witness for your husband," she said, lowering her voice. "So, no, I won't be."

On one evening, while Lorkens and I were at home, (and our children were in bed), my husband came up really close to me. I was standing or walking.

"You're crazy," Lorkens said, standing in front of me. Lorkens was 5 feet and 9 and a quarter of an inch in height, while I was 5 feet and 7.75 inches in height. We were near the front door of our condo unit. "You're crazy. You're crazy. You're crazy. You're crazy. You're crazy. You're crazy. You're crazy." I exited the home and sat on the floor where the black stairs were located. This was near the front door. Then, after a bit, I returned inside our home.

At another moment, he was behaving in a controlling manner. Moreover, he was not behaving in a respectful manner towards my son. My son said something in a low voice to him, while they were at the front door of the condo unit. Then, my husband said to repeat it.

"I love you!" my son said. His face was about two inches from his dad's face.

"No!" Lorkens said. "What did you say? Repeat it." Then, he repeated what he had said.

"You said the truth," I said to my son. "That's good."

"Don't interfere," Lorkens said to me.

"You won't go outside with me, if you don't repeat it," Lorkens said. Then, Junior said, "I love you."

"No, that's not what you said," Lorkens said.

"I don't know what you want me to say," Lorkens Junior said. I spoke to my husband briefly about the matter, and I was defending my son.

"Don't interfere," Lorkens said. "I don't interfere with what you say to your children in the bathroom. So, don't interfere." *That's not true*, I thought.

"Go to your room," Lorkens said. "Come on, baby," Lorkens said to Soraya. "Let's go." They headed out immediately while my son was crying terribly and went to his bedroom. I yelled some type of scolding remark from the doorway at Lorkens as he departed from our condo unit with our daughter. Soraya and her dad went outside for a walk together. I joined my son in the bedroom and held his body. Nevertheless, he moved it this way and that. So, I let his body go. He was in bed, but he was punching his bed. I told him comforting words, but he continued to cry. The crying persisted for an hour in his bedroom.

His father came home. Then, he commanded his son to not exit his bedroom until I finished the preparation of his dish for supper.

"Lorkens, may I let Junior out of his room now?" I said subsequent to the hour that had elapsed. "It's been an hour." Lorkens Junior's supper was not fully cooked yet.

"Yes," he said. I quickly walked down the hallway and unlocked Junior's bedroom door.

"You may come out now," I said.

On a separate day, I was in the kitchen. My daughter had been acting up since she returned home (after missing her usual resting time and snack time). I kept a schedule for all the children to follow, and I honoured that schedule. Nevertheless, the father had not honoured it. She had gone out with her dad, so she was behaving in a moody manner. Then, I commanded her to head to bed.

"Soraya's becoming like Dad," Junior said, while she was heading to her bedroom.

"How could you say such a thing about your dad?" Lorkens said to Junior. Then, he was going on about it, saying, "I can't believe that… I will send you to a psychologist." Then, Junior started bawling. Junior ran to me.

"My mom will protect me," Junior said.

"Let's go to the washroom," I said. My husband forbade us from speaking to each other in private. Then, I entered Junior's bedroom with my son, and my husband prevented me from locking the door. He came into the bedroom, where we were situated. He forbade me from speaking to my son without him there.

"Please, let me speak to my son in private," I said. "I'm his mom."

"No," he said. Then, he threatened to call the police.

"I'm scared," my son said. "I'm scared of him." So, I called my dad. My husband said that I was bringing my children to conduct themselves like that. Then, I departed from our condo unit with my son. We descended the staircase all the way down to the ground. Then, we came to the front of another condo unit and walked to the side of it. I wanted to comfort him, so I took my son in my arms.

"Forgive your dad," I said. I asked my son about the bath that his dad gave him with Soraya. I asked him about the temperature of the water.

"It was like lava," he said, while I recorded him in audio-visual form on my cell phone. Then, we re-entered into our condo unit.

"I did not want to do the forgiveness, because I did not want you to go to jail," Junior said later on. I had been teaching him certain steps of forgiveness in his bedroom, that I had learned from my mentor.

Soraya slept a long time in her bed before exiting her bedroom.

On many occasions while living in Gatineau, when Lorkens Senior would give Soraya and Junior a bath, he would be about to pour water on them and they would jump out of the way before it fell on them. This indicated that the temperature of the water was indecent.

"Was the water too hot?" I asked Soraya.

"It was very cold," she said.

I rebuked my husband on this matter. Nevertheless, he did not obey my command.

I aimed to talk to my husband about matters in private and away from our children. Nevertheless, when I did so, he refused to enter a room to talk in private about matters. So, I ended up talking to him in their presence. On one of these occasions, Soraya cried, and slid against the wall onto the floor. I hugged her, but she did not enjoy the hug. So, I released my hold on her.

On the first day of preschool (maternelle 4 ans) for Soraya, my husband was making an issue with the container. It was August. I had notified him that I had not put Soraya's container in the backpack. I had placed it in the fridge the night before that morning.

"I checked the backpack," he said. I told him a second time that it was located in the fridge. He took another container and put some food in it. I gave him the container that I had inserted into the fridge the night before.

"Here's the container," I said.

"What did you say?" he asked me.

"Do you want the container or not?" I said. "I don't want to argue." He was acting hostile that morning. Before then, I had commanded him to keep it down twice, because he had been raising his voice.

"What?" he had said. Then, he acted as if I was fabricating a lie. It was almost 7 a.m. by that time.

Later on in the day, Lorkens was placing toy after toy into a big, black garbage bag. I contested with him over this repetitive action, because he had dropped so many toys into the garbage bag. There were almost no toys left.

"Why are you throwing out all these toys?" I said.

"You threw out toys," he said to me. "So, I'm doing the same." Yes, I had disposed of three toys. Nevertheless, there was a great amount of toys that still remained in the place.

"May we still keep the chick toy for Eve?" I said.

"Yes," he said. Then, there were almost no toys remaining in our residence outside of this garbage bag. About 20 toys were disposed of in this bag.

"You're throwing all the toys out," my son said. "We have to follow the rule." Then, Lorkens sent his son to his bedroom for over an hour.

My husband played the king.

"You shall not have anything else for breakfast after you eat this soup," he said to the children and I. They were staying at home for the entire day and were physically ill. Now, he was restricting them from certain items of food. My daughter, Soraya, was asking for porridge after she finished eating her soup.

"May I give them fruits or vegetables for breakfast?" I asked my husband.

"No," he said.

Then, at snack time, I gave my children their Lara bar halves and a bunch of nuts.

"Don't give them oily foods," he said. He removed their nuts and Lara bar halves and placed some fruit on the table as a snack. *He is acting controlling with the children,* I thought. This was the customary way in which he treated us. If one member of his household did not submit to his control, he would lose his cool. He would behave in a scornful and hateful manner, and he would attempt to shame that person.

I habitually told Soraya to put on her bedtime clothing at night. Then, I would put her into her bed at bedtime. Her twin bed was enclosed by posts and a bed rail. Her outfit consisted of some pajamas or a nightgown. If she wanted another blanket and Eve nor Junior was using it, I would give it to her. That was contingent on whether it was a blanket that was big enough for her body or not. Nevertheless, at one point, my husband started to have Soraya go to bed almost naked. He would command her to skip putting on warm clothing (after changing out of her daytime clothing) even though she would request it. She also asked for a blanket and was denied another one oftentimes by her dad. Nevertheless, it was autumn.

One time in particular, my husband commanded Soraya to remove her clothes right before bedtime. So, Soraya removed her pyjamas, but she still wore her panty. Then, she got into her bed at night, and her dad closed the door. A little while afterwards, she opened her bedroom door. She requested a certain, furry vest. I was holding it, and Soraya ran to me.

"You're still up?" Lorkens said. I handed her the vest. "Put the jacket back." She returned it to me and cried noisily while heading to her bedroom. She was crying in the bedroom where Eve slept. She went to bed, wearing only a pink panty and it was cool outside on that night. So, a little while afterwards, I concealed the furry vest under my clothing. Then, I headed to her bedroom, and I handed her the furry vest while she was in her bedroom.

"Thank you," she said. She sat up, and she embraced me. Moreover, she kissed my cheek.

On a separate day, I placed many cashews on our dining room table. Then, I asked Lorkens to tend to the children. (I had gotten up at around 5 a.m., and I had not had 7 hours in bed overnight but, rather, only about 5 and a half hours. Eve had woken up at around 5:15 a.m. crying. So, I had tended to her and had risen since then.) Then, my children consumed an orange and their dad said to not eat anymore. He was supposed to offer them some soup. Soraya was hungry as she watched for some food. She grasped some food, but her dad took it from her. He commanded her to watch for her soup.

"She's hungry," I said. "Why don't you give her something?" She was crying after he removed it from her hands.

"Go," he said. "Do your thing." Then, I headed to our bedroom, and I lay down on our bed.

There were occasions (when I did not submit to my husband), when I should have submitted myself to him. Sometimes, I sympathized with my children, and I obeyed them instead of him. Moreover, I revealed favouritism towards Soraya over our other children, and he displayed favouritism towards her over our other children, as well. I started to show her favouritism after my husband began doing so. In the beginning, I rebuked the behaviour, but eventually I was unwillingly giving into it.

In 2021, on one day, I entered the washroom and closed the door. Then, I fastened it.

"God, I need your help!" I whispered. "I don't know how much longer I can do this for." I had been tending to the children for years. I did not have holidays off. Moreover, I did not have a day off from watching out for my children, even on Mother's Day. From birth, I was their caregiver, while Lorkens habitually stayed in his bedroom with his door shut. So, I was taking care of them, while they were awake, until they went to bed at night. There were no breaks to catch up on sleep that my husband allotted to me (even if I was breastfeeding during the night). Oftentimes, if my husband caught me taking a break, he would bark out orders. I thought that he did not permit breaks once I gave birth to my first child, Lorkens Junior. That was when these orders started coming during my breaks. It was an overtime shift daily. So, I searched for opportunities to rest, and did rest at times. Moreover, the pressure from my husband, our neighbour and my husband's emotional abuse were really hard to endure. Each evening, my soul was fragmenting from no quality time with my husband. I watched for the moment when he would ask me day after day to spend some quality time with him. So, there were some evenings, when I cried over this neglect.

Around mid-September to the first day of October, my husband said to me, "Tell me when you're going crazy." *This is all a game to him*, I thought.

On a separate day, my husband said, "There will be an emergency court session for you. You will be sent to a place for crazy people."

On a certain autumn day, while our children, my husband and I were at home, two women entered our residence. My mom was not present. One of them was a tall, blond-haired woman, who grinned at me. One of them asked us when we could meet them at a certain location.

« Après que je nourrisse mon bébé, je serai disponible, » I said. *After I nourish my baby, I will be available.*

« C'est quand que vous nourrissez votre bébé? » the blond-haired woman said. *When do you feed your baby?*

« À 16h, » I said. *At 4 p.m.* She ordered me to come after I feed my baby. A certain location was determined and the two women left our home. After I fed Eve with some solid food, we headed out to the location in a minivan. My husband drove the red minivan with our children in tow and I in it. We exited the minivan on a hot, sunny day. I wore pink sunglasses. We filed into a waiting room and sat on chairs. When it was our turn, Lorkens Senior went into the room, shutting the door. I heard him saying the word, 'she,' in an accusative tone of voice multiple times, while the children sat near me. We were waiting in the reception area. Following an hour, the door opened, and my husband exited the room. One of the ladies invited me into the room, and I entered it. Then, I closed the door. The blond-haired woman interrogated me, while the brunette took notes. The brunette was Camille. She had dark brown, chin-length hair. I honestly answered her queries. Moreover, I did not hold a thing back.

The blond-haired lady said that she was concerned about two matters. One of those things was that my children were learning about demons so young," she said. The other matter is not to be revealed here, because God wants me to omit that detail.

"I am concerned that the father –" I said. I do not want to include the rest of the sentence here in this book.

This happened five minutes into the interrogation.

"You can only speak to your children while being monitored by children's services," one of the women said. I exited the room.

"I can only speak to my children while being monitored," I loudly announced to my children in the waiting area. I was in shock. Then, I looked at the woman at the reception desk and she gave me a cold, uncompassionate stare.

While my husband accompanied the children, I descended the staircase, since the blond-haired lady desired that I do so. I stayed at the bottom of the stairs and quietly teared up. Then, I put on my sunglasses. The lady met me there. Then, Lorkens Senior and our children entered the car. I approached the minivan.

"Goodbye, Junior," I said, approaching him. "Goodbye, Soraya," I said, approaching her. "Goodbye, Eve," I said.

"Goodbye!" Junior and Soraya said. Then, my husband drove the minivan away from the building and out of my view.

Then, the same two women entered a sedan, and, then, I penetrated it. The blond-haired woman drove the sedan to the street of my home. The lady parked the car on the spot almost right in front of our condo unit's lawn.

"You have two options," the blond-haired lady said. "You leave, or they leave."

"So, I have to move out, or they have to move out?" I said.

"Yes," she replied. "You move out, or they find another place to live."

"I'll go," I said. "I'll move out."

"Do you want to go to your mom's place or your dad's place?" she said.

"My dad's place," I said.

"You have ten minutes to pack your stuff," she said. I exited the car and turned the silver key. Then, I opened the front door. My husband and our children exited the home. With the front door shut, I heard one of my children crying audibly. I packed my stuff in a suitcase and silently teared up. Then, I heard someone beating the front door. So, I opened it.

"Yes?" I said.

"10 minutes are up," the blonde said. "It's time to leave."

"Okay," I said and closed the door. I packed some additional stuff, and, then, I heard someone, beating the same door. I gathered my belongings and pulled my red suitcase to the door. "Je suis prête," I said. *I am ready.*

"Goodbye, Junior!" I said. I embraced him. He was five years young. Junior had black hair. He possessed light brown skin and brown eyes.

"Goodbye, Soraya!" I said, and I held her in my arms. Soraya had curly, blond hair at that point. She had a slight tan to her skin, which made it look orange. Soraya was four years young. I felt like I was going to cry, if I would say, "Goodbye!" to Eve. Eve was fifteen months young. So, I did not embrace her nor say a word to her. If I had cried in my father's presence, my father would treat me angrily and abusively and/or ignore me. I walked over to the car. I waved to her from inside the car, and I intended to say, "Bye, Eve!" in an audible voice from inside the car.

Nevertheless, when I pressed the button to lower the window, it did not descend. The window was locked. Then, the blond-haired lady drove the car away from my residence. The brunette was sitting in the front passenger seat. She was somewhat stocky with chin-length hair. The blonde dropped me off in the parking lot in front of my dad's home.

I pulled my suitcase out of the trunk, and I grasped the bottom of it with my hand. Then, I lowered it to the ground. I pulled the suitcase across the parking lot and along the sidewalk. Then, I plodded up the steps to my dad's condo unit, and he opened the front door.

"Oh, Sandy!" he said in a compassionate tone of voice. He closed the door, and he opened his arms wide. I embraced him, bursting into tears. 'Where are they? Oh, they're taking off now, trying to get away before I see them. I would have asked them, "Why are you doing this"? if they hadn't just torn off. Did they help you with your suitcase?'

"No," I said.

I brought my luggage and backpack down the staircase, and to my bedroom. Then, I removed many objects from my suitcase. I typed a message to Nicole through the Message app on my black iPad.

"Send a message to Joy right away," she texted me. So, I dispatched an e-mail to Joy.

A little while afterwards, Joy initiated a Zoom session with Nicole and I. On that evening, I greeted them.

"I'm disappointed in you, Sandra," Joy said. "You should not have left." Joy possessed medium brown skin, black hair, and shiny, white teeth. I cried, turning my face away from the video camera. "What is it with white women?" Then, she stated that white women have passivity.

"Not me," Nicole said. Nicole was a Caucasian.

"What should I have done?" I said.

"I would not let anyone take me away from my children," Joy said. "I would not leave without some blood being drawn."

"Oh," I said. "You would not have left unless some blood was drawn."

"You got to go back tomorrow," Joy said. "Go back to your home tomorrow." I verbally concurred to what she had commanded. Then, she executed deliverance on me.

On the following morning, I attended a court session in Québec. It was at the Chambre De Jeunesse in the Palais de Justice. The same notetaker (from the day before that day) was the accuser of mine in the court room. She was a member of the DYP in Québec. In French, it is called the DPJ. The judge ordered that I should be supervised if I go to my residence, because the children dwelt there. The brunette was a social worker. She said that the supervision measures may be lifted soon.

Homeward Bound

At about 5:15 p.m., I reached the front door of my former home. I unlocked the door with my key. Then, I entered the condo unit. There was not a single person in view. I pulled my suitcase inside. Then, Lorkens Junior exited the washroom. His soul looked like it was dead. When he came out, he looked like he had become overheated. He looked like he was exhausted. Nevertheless, he was neither overheated nor exhausted. One by one each child came out of the bathroom and, lastly, my mom came out of the bathroom. My children and I spoke to each other. Then, I started to get Eve's supper ready. My husband reached his home, and he immediately called the DYP. He passed the phone to me, and she asked me twice to depart. I firmly responded, "No" following the request both times.

Two policemen entered Lorkens' condo unit. They spoke with me, and our children were sent out of the room. One of the policemen continuously repeated the court order on that day from the judge. Moreover, he repeated the consequences, that he said would happen as a result of contempt of court. They queried me why I did not depart. One of them asked me why I had returned. This man had come on the other occasion, when Lorkens had called the police. This man was playing the role of a policeman instead of a crisis intervention worker. He was wearing the typical policeman uniform. Eve was sitting in her booster seat, which was on a white chair. I put Eve's supper on her divided tray, and I placed this tray onto the wooden table. Then, I placed Eve into her high chair. She started to pick up her food pieces, and, then, she put them into her mouth.

« Qu'est-ce que tu vas faire? » he said. *What are you going to do?*

« Je vais nourrir mon enfant et le mettre au lit, » I said. *I will nourish my child and put it to bed.* The black-haired policeman kept accusing me of having triggered something in the future. They alluded to it with the word, "this" or the like in French. « Ce n'est pas ma faute, » I said.

I heard my mother telling a policeman that I am very stubborn.

"Your mother did not know that you'd come inside the home," the policeman said.

Eve finished her meal. So, I removed her from her high chair, and I brought her to the white-tiled washroom. I examined Eve's diaper and handled it. It was dry. So, I slipped her brown, long-sleeved onesie on her.

"Good night, sweetheart!" I said to her. "I love you! God bless you." Then, I gently placed her in her white crib. She was one year and five months old. She lay down in her bed. Then, I left the bedroom and returned to the dining room.

The man with jet black hair repetitively said "tête de cochon." That means pig's head. People use that French term to indicate that someone is stubborn. Then, the other policeman commanded him to lay off. So, he stopped repeating that expression. The policeman with jet black hair muttered something under his breath.

A DYP woman entered my husband's dwelling. She had chin-length, blond hair. She appeared to have lived about 55 years. She threatened to take the children with her to a foster home, if I would not leave their place. I overheard my mom making a crying sound in the bathroom. Then, my mom besought me to reside at her apartment.

"No," I said. Then, my mom said to the DYP lady that she would lead the children to her residence. The DYP lady agreed to that. So, my mom took the playpen.

"I knew that you would call the police," Junior said, looking at his dad.

"I did not call the police," Lorkens said. This is the same reply that Lorkens Senior had retorted to me earlier on that day.

"He did not call the police," I said. "He called the DPJ, and they called the police." I had bought into his father's fabricated story. I was just reiterating what Lorkens Senior had stated. I handed the black bag for the playpen to my mom, and she left with our children. My husband left, too, and headed to the red minivan. Then, he drove off with the children and my mom in tow. Then, the police exited the residence.

Separation

My mentor, Joy, did approve of what I had executed on that day in which I had returned to my home in Gatineau, Québec.

On the following day, when Lorkens Senior passed the cell phone to me (while I was still at our condo unit in Québec), Luc let me communicate with my children through the cell phone. I was seated at a black dining table. Then, I greeted my mom over the phone.

"I can't talk to you," she said. "The DPJ lady told me not to talk to you nor let you talk to the children." The judge had neither told me before nor told me afterwards that communicating with my mom was forbidden.

My husband threw a celebration for himself at one point after initiating the divorce proceedings in court. After my return to his place, he almost never looked at me: including any part of me.

The brown-haired social worker of the DYP arrived at Lorkens' dwelling three days afterwards.

"You're going to have to leave," she said. "The children can't stay with their grandma." Her name was Camille. She departed from our condo unit through the doorway. A little bit of time afterwards, I called my dad on my MagicJack phone. I requested that he bring me to his home once more. I told him what had transpired with the social worker on that very day. On the following day, I spotted my dad's white car through the side window. We were at the end unit. Then, I exited the condo unit and bolted the door. I brought my luggage to his white car. I placed it in his trunk. Nevertheless, I placed my purse on my lap and sat in the front passenger seat. Then, we headed to my dad's brick condo unit, as my dad drove the car.

On another day, I attended a contempt of court session at the Chambre De Jeunesse. It is a courtroom that is dedicated to the DYP. The blond-haired judge ordered that I only have access to my children under the supervision of the DYP every week. She recommended that I meet up with my children once a week.

Two weeks after my encounter with my children at that condo unit (in which they were taken away), I went to the DYP center and met up with my children for the first appointment. We spent an hour and a half with each other. Each one of them cried at the end of the visit, when it was the time of departure. So, I rushed up to one after another to hug and comfort each one.

Subsequently, they returned home with their dad by minivan. One monitored visit continued to occur weekly at the same center and was monitored by one or two DYP staff members. During these visits, the DYP supervisor or supervisors continually typed or wrote throughout each visit.

Two weeks afterwards, the visit of mine with my children at this center was cancelled. The brown-haired social worker said that the children had pneumonia and were in the hospital. *They do not have pneumonia*, God informed me.

"Lorkens Junior has asthma, Lorkens told me," my dad said in another month. That was false, too. I knew that, for God made that clear.

Near the exact middle of November of that same year, just a bit before noon, our doorbell rang. I heard loud knocking on the front door. I unclosed the front door and a policeman and a policewoman greeted me.

"May we come in or do you want us to talk outside?" the man said.

"You may come inside," I said.

"I understand that your children have been taken away," the woman said. I felt intense anger come over me, but I was holding it in. I could feel my face shaking.

"Would you, please, lay off of me?" I said. "I'm in the process of getting a divorce." She started questioning about my personal life.

"Are you thinking suicidal thoughts?" she said.

"No," I said.

"How is your sleep lately?" she said.

"Good," I said.

"Are you on medication?" the policewoman said.

"No," I said." Are you on medication?"

"No," she said.

"That's enough questions about my personal life," I said. Then, at the end, she gave me mental health cards.

"Or, if we leave, and you think you need help, you can call these numbers," she said. They departed from our home and I was at home solo again.

After my dad came home, I informed him of what had occurred in his absence. So, he called my mom, but he did not get ahold of her. Then, she called him back.

"Why did you call the police?" my father said on the phone.

"I wanted Sandy to get help," my mother said.

"Did something happen lately, or is it just a general concern?" Dad said.

"Just a general concern," Mom said.

Fifteen days afterwards, my dad's cell phone rang, as we were entering Loblaws.

"Do you know where she is?" the person said. This person was questioning my dad.

"She's right beside me," Dad said.

"Do you mean, she's at 52 or 53?" the man said.

"We're at Loblaws, shopping," Dad said. "It's the police." He passed me the iPhone. I laughed. I exited the store and went outdoors.

"Hello," I said.

"How are you?" the policeman said.

"I'm fine," I said. "How are you?"

"Your mom called us, telling us that you were threatening to kill yourself," the policeman said.

"I did not threaten to kill myself," I said. "That is not true. Why does she keep calling the police? She did this last week; I don't live with her. I don't talk to her. How would she know?"

"Did you talk to her today?" he said.

"No, and I did not talk to her yesterday either," I said.

"Are you okay?" the policeman said.

"I'm fine, sir," I said. Then, we uttered our goodbyes and the call ended.

Towards the end of the same year, I asked Camille, the brunette, if I may undertake phone calls with my children. She permitted me do so while a DYP member monitored each phone conversation. Moreover, I had weekly monitored visits with my children at the center. During two of these visits, my son begged me at the end of the visit to bring him home. I denied him this. The judge had not permitted me to do so, I replied. So, he was crying, and, then, he dragged himself off of the floor. He walked down the hallway all the way to where his dad was standing. His dad was standing at the door at the end of that hallway.

On one day, a private investigator called me. She desired to meet up with me to get further information. I asked God in my head, *Should I go?* God replied, "Do not go." So, I refused to have such a meeting with her.

I discovered a criminal lawyer by phone. He queried me if I had participated in an interview with the private investigator.

« Non, » I said. *No*.

« C'est bon, » he said. *That's good*. He told me to meet up with the private investigator. He instructed me to not give her information about what occurred.

So, I fixed an appointment with the private investigator at the police station. Then, some days afterwards, at the appointment, I signed a sheet of paper. The lady opened the door for me and let me depart. I met up with my dad in his car. Then, he drove off from the police station, and tears ran down my cheeks.

"The lady said that I'm not allowed to see Junior nor Soraya," I said, while I sat in the front passenger seat. He was in shock.

I continued to see Eve at the Centre Multi-Services Jeunesse as the DYP monitored us behind a screen of glass. They continually took notes as we spent quality time together.

In February of 2022, I attended a court session at the Chambre De Jeunesse. My mom appeared online in a video, testifying against me. On the following day, God told me that it did not make sense that I desired to talk to my mom on the phone.

"This is crazy," he said. "You're talking to her after she called the police, reporting a false story against you, and she witnessed against you in court falsely." I was occasionally talking to her at that time. (Moreover, before God exposed her sabotage to me in 2020 and in 2021, I was her very close friend.) Nevertheless, since God told me so, at that moment, I decided to stop conversing with my mom on the phone. I decided to refrain from talking to her altogether anymore from that point on.

On a weekly basis, my dad bought me so many things that I requested. This happened while I established my residence at his place. I was grateful for his generosity. In general, I did not work, because people were not hiring me. When I did find an opportunity (in which someone was willing to pay me for work), I worked.

By the way, God taught me how to manage my money, while I was residing at my father's condo unit. God provided me with a credit card, that was not under anyone else's name for the first time. God gave me more financial freedom. Certain things were permitted that would not have been permitted without that freedom.

Nevertheless, from the afternoon up to the evening, my dad would drink a great quantity of alcohol. My father commonly practiced emotional abuse towards me. Sometimes, I reacted in a passive-aggressive manner. For example, I would look at him angrily or develop hate in my heart towards him. Or I would rarely swear while unaccompanied in my bedroom sometimes. I did not trust him.

The distrust in my heart stemmed from much trauma throughout my life, which brought me to develop suspicion towards people in general.

Moreover, I did not believe that people loved me. I believed that everyone hated me.

Deliverance

In October, I had a personal session with my mentor on Zoom. Her name was Anne Latour. She possessed blond hair and tanned skin and a round forehead.

"I've been experiencing choking fits every six months or so, while I'd be eating and have to spit out my food to prevent choking to death," I said. Then, she started to interrogate my soul fragments. I was astonished by what God revealed and did during the session. After the deliverance session, I no longer had long choking fits with teary eyes while I consumed food.

On the 31st day of October, I had a one-on-one session with my mentor, Anne, once more. Jesus was part of the session. He healed my personal soul fragments from the event in which my children and I initially were separated from each other by two members of the DYP. Afterwards, I was no longer crying daily from the trauma of that day.

In November of 2023, there was a court session with my lawyer. She was my divorce and DYP lawyer. She possessed long, wavy, dark hair.

Neither did I show up nor was I required to show up for it. It took place at the Chambre De Jeunesse.

On the following morning, I excitedly called her on the phone.

"The criminal court judge made a declaration," Noha solemnly said. "She declared that you are allowed to see all three of your children under the supervision of the DPJ." The DPJ is the French name for the Director of Youth Protection in Québec. I was orally rejoicing over this with my lawyer, but she did not share my enthusiasm. Then, the phone call ended. I dashed up the stairs.

"I'm allowed to see all three of my children now!" I told my dad.

"That's great!" my dad said, and he gave me a hug. "I'm really looking forward to seeing you guys be reunited with each other!"

"Yeah!" I said. "It'll be great!"

In April of 2023, I arrived in front of the Centre Multi-Services Jeunesse in Hull, Québec and watched for my children. I was standing there, and I held my big, grey purse and a red tote bag. The area was really sunny. I put my bags down. Soraya came out of a car, and she spotted me. Her hips and legs went into Sonic the Hedgehog mode. She bolted as fast as she could towards me. I bent down and kneeled. Then, my son exited the car, and started running towards me. She hugged me, and I hugged her. Then, my son wrapped his arms around me as soon as he arrived at my side. I embraced him.

Lessons of Mine

Relationships

First and foremost, your relationship must be God-ordained. If God did not tell you to wed that person, do not wed that person. Moreover, do not enter a romantic relationship with that individual. What is the point? Your heart will simply get broken.

Therefore, if you do not discern God's voice, or you do not perceive how to discern His voice, you must discover how to do so. It is critical to your well-being and the well-being of your children.

Getting along well does not mean that the other person necessarily cares about your well-being. Lust and/or malice could still be lurking behind that person's mask.

If a guy does not change according to your desires before your wedding, do not rely on that change after your wedding ceremony. It may never occur. If you rely on that to make your marriage healthy, it is not wise. You may end up making a big mistake, and you may have to suffer from it day after day. First and foremost, it must be a God-destined marriage. If God did not tell you to wed that person, do not wed that person. There are people who have evil intentions for their spouse. Marriage does not necessarily equal godly love.

Ouija Boards

The Ouija board appears to be a toy, but it is far from it. Ouija boards are a way to communicate with evil spirits. These evil spirits are not dead, loved ones as some suppose. They are part of the kingdom of darkness, and they are spiritual beings. They are in the spirit realm. Ouija boards frequently have been used in séances with a medium. Even though (when I was using the Ouija board) I was not conducting a séance and there was no medium, it still resulted in answers that did not stem from God. Even though I did not believe that a dead person was going to answer my question through the Ouija board, nor was I seeking to speak to dead people with it, it was still a cursed object. The Bible says, "There shall not be found among you anyone that maketh his son or his daughter to pass through this fire, or that useth divination, or an observer of times, or an enchanter, or a witch, Or a charmer, or a consulter with familiar spirits, or a wizard, or a necromancer. For all that do these things are an abomination unto the LORD: and because of these abominations the LORD thy God doth drive them out from before thee" (Deuteronomy 18:10-12). Moreover, the Holy Bible says, "And when they shall say unto you, Seek unto them that have familiar spirits, and unto wizards that peep, and that mutter: should not a people seek unto their God? For the living to the dead? To the law and to the testimony: if they speak not according to this word, it is because there is no light in them" (Isaiah 8:19-20). The Bible says the following about cursed objects, "The graven images of their gods shall ye burn with fire: thou shalt not desire the silver or gold that is on them, nor take it unto thee, lest thou be snared therein: for it is an abomination to the LORD thy God. Neither shalt thou bring an abomination into thine house lest thou be a cursed thing like it: but thou shalt utterly detest it, and thou shalt utterly abhor it; for it is a cursed thing" (Deuteronomy 7:25-26). God does not want a cursed thing to be in one's home.

Yoga

Yoga is not innocent, as many people make it appear. It is attached to a religion: Hinduism. Moreover, it may cause depression, spasms, and other negative side effects. I do not recommend yoga to people. A former yoga instructor expounds on this topic some more in the cited video from the YouTube channel, Reign. The former yoga instructor's name is Steve Bancarz.

Automatic writing

Automatic writing is a tool of the Devil. It is also called a stream of consciousness. It is being used to lead people to believe that they will improve their writing through this activity. It is actually the process of demons, who are taking control of your arm. The demons bring you to write things. They inspire ideas that do not originate from the person's mind. Automatic writing is done very hastily. It is not a pre-planned form of writing. It is an impromptu form of writing, in which the person does not necessarily know what he/she will write next.

Narcissism

I have seen much narcissism in my life and been subject to narcissistic abuse. I would like to, therefore, expound on narcissism. I found some information on it from the following source. Her name was Angel. She studied the DSM-5 in her psychiatry course and described narcissism from this manual in detail. You may check out her video; the URL is on the page, Works Cited, at the back of this book. Moreover, you may discover more about other possible narcissistic behaviour from another woman, if you check the page, Works Cited, in this book. Not every narcissist is going to behave in the same manner. Moreover, there are covert narcissists. Nevertheless, all of them have some things in common, that Angel deals with. There is a lack of empathy and a lack of accountability. So, if you seek to correct the person on their behaviour, they claim that you are the issue. They do not generally desire to ameliorate their behaviour in a single shape or form. There are exceptions, but they are not the general pattern. If you dwell with them, you will notice this pattern. There tends to be gaslighting, as well. I am basing my perception off of my experience with many narcissists. Since I lived with one or more during almost my whole life, I am expounding on the topic. Moreover, God wants me to shed light on this matter.

Epilogue

I grew up in an environment of abuse in which people gaslit me. Therefore, I accepted lies from the enemy (Satan). I did not trust my instincts and was easily swayed by others. My gullibility led me to reenter a romantic relationship with Lorkens. His guilt-tripping convinced me. He played the victim, fooling me.

What we do can impact us for a lifetime and in the hereafter. This is why the acceptance of Jesus as our Lord and Saviour is so vital. "All have sinned and come short of the glory of God" (Romans 3:23, KJV). "For the wages of sin is death; but the gift of God is eternal life through Jesus Christ our Lord" (Romans 6:23). "For God so loved the world, that he gave his only begotten Son, that whosoever believeth in him should not perish, but have everlasting life" (John 3:16). The Son of God is King Jesus. He died for your sins. He paid the penalty with His life to give you everlasting life and not perish. This salvation is conditional. If you neither believe in nor trust in Jesus, you will not be saved. You will end up in hell forever. Nevertheless, if you trust in Jesus, you will be saved. This means that you accept Him as the Lord and Saviour of your soul. Moreover, in the latter case, you will have eternal life in heaven. "We love him, because he first loved us" (1 John 4:19).

Works Cited

The Reign. "The Dangers of Yoga." *YouTube*. 2019. 12 Jul. 2022.

<https://www.youtube.com/watch?v=uIPCoFIM0XI>

Anjel Speaks. "What Is A Narcissist? According To The DSM-5 And The Bible." *YouTube*. 2017. 24 Aug. 2020.
<https://www.youtube.com/watch?v=NB2FqXIkD2I&t=919s>

Bradley, Michael. "The Dangers of Automatic Writing." Web page. 24 Aug. 2023. 2024.

<https://www.bible-knowledge.com/dangers-of-automatic-writing/>

www.ingramcontent.com/pod-product-compliance
Lightning Source LLC
Chambersburg PA
CBHW051755230426
43670CB00012B/2297